Contents

Acknowledgements

The text used for the poems in this edition is that of the Oxford Authors *Gerard Manley Hopkins* volume edited by Catherine Phillips.

In preparing this new edition of Hopkins's selected poems in the Oxford Student Texts series I have benefited from the guidance and advice of Dr Victor Lee and Jan Doorly. In addition, Jenny Roberts has exercised a judicious and supportive editorial hand in seeing the text through to publication. I would also like to record my indebtedness to Lucy Hooper of Oxford University Press, who saw through to publication the two earlier editions of this selection.

Editors

Dr Victor Lee, the series editor, read English at University College, Cardiff. He was later awarded his doctorate at the University of Oxford. He has taught at secondary and tertiary level, working at the Open University for 27 years. Victor Lee's experience as an examiner is very wide. He has been, for example, a Chief Examiner in English A level for three different boards, stretching over a period of more than 30 years.

Dr Peter Feeney read English and Theology at Clare College Cambridge, going on to complete a doctoral thesis on links between Theology and Tragedy. He has taught English at comprehensive schools in Leicestershire, Suffolk and Northampton, as well as acting as examiner and chief moderator at AS and A level in English Literature. More recently he has managed A level and GCSE provision at Suffolk College in Ipswich as head of its Tertiary A Level centre. He is currently on secondment to the Suffolk 14–19 Strategy, where his principal role involves working with a group of school sixth forms, FE colleges and work-based training providers, as post-16 improvement adviser.

Foreword

Oxford Student Texts are specifically aimed at presenting poetry and drama to an audience studying English literature at an advanced level. Each text is designed as an integrated whole consisting of four main parts. The first part sets the scene by discussing the context in which the work was written. The most important part of the book is the poetry or play itself, and it is suggested that the student read this first without consulting the Notes or other secondary sources. To encourage students to follow this advice, the Notes are placed together after the text, not alongside it. Where help is needed, the Notes and Interpretations sections provide it.

The Notes perform two functions. First, they provide information and explain allusions. Second (this is where they differ from most texts at this level), they often raise questions of central concern to the interpretation of the poems or play being dealt with, particularly in the general note placed at the beginning of each set of notes.

The fourth part, the Interpretations section, deals with major issues of response to the particular selection of poetry or drama. One of the major aims of this part of the text is to emphasize that there is no one right answer to interpretation, but a series of approaches. Readers are given guidance as to what counts as evidence, but in the end left to make up their own minds as to which are the most suitable interpretations, or to add their own.

In these revised editions, the Interpretations section now addresses a wider range of issues. There is a more detailed treatment of context and critical history, for example. The section contains a number of activity-discussion sequences, although it must be stressed that these are optional. Significant issues about the poetry or play are raised, and readers are invited to tackle activities before proceeding to the discussion section, where possible responses to the questions raised are considered. Their main function is to engage readers actively in the ideas of the text.

At the end of each text there is also a list of Essay Questions. Whereas the activity-discussion sequences are aimed at increasing understanding of the literary work itself, these tasks are intended to help explore ideas about the poetry or play after the student has completed the reading of the work and the studying of the Notes and Interpretations. These tasks are particularly helpful for coursework projects or in preparing for an examination.

Victor Lee *Series Editor*

Hopkins the Jesuit priest in 1879: this dates from his time as a parish priest in Oxford and Liverpool. The sonnet *Felix Randal* (p. 45) draws powerfully on his experiences in that vocation.

Gerard Manley Hopkins in Context

The 'context' in which a writer operates involves many different layers. The approach adopted here makes a simple distinction between the external world (contemporary developments in literature, science and thought, for instance) and Hopkins's rich internal world, the activity of his mind as powerfully illuminated by the prose of his letters, Journal entries, sermons and devotional writings. You will find these writings referred to here in the Context section and later, both in the Interpretations section and in the notes provided for individual poems. From them we can build up a better sense of the personality that informs the poetry, just as from looking at wider cultural developments we can better relate Hopkins's concerns as a writer to some of the dominant themes in his contemporary world.

The external context

From the start it is worth stressing that the life and the poems are vitally connected by a factor that makes Hopkins unusual for (even antagonistic to) the era in which he lived. The most basic fact any reading of Hopkins's poetry will provide is that its author had deeply held religious beliefs. The second half of the nineteenth century – the period in which Hopkins lived – saw belief as a central feature of the common culture steadily declining. 'Secularism' – the idea that society does not need religious values to maintain order or provide meaning – had been a growing feature of life among the educated classes of Europe for over 100 years when Hopkins was born in 1844. As science found more effective hypotheses for explaining the underlying organization of the natural world (and in so doing achieved progressively greater predictive capacity about the shape of future events), and technology developed reliable devices for controlling the physical environment to make it safer, more convenient and more comfortable than ever before, so religion as a device for explaining the world became displaced from the central role it had once played.

At the heart of secularism was the belief that moral, legal and civil codes – the ground rules and shared assumptions by which people lived in social organizations, solved disputes and defined themselves – could be satisfactorily established and sustained through human reason. There was no need to look beyond reason to a divine law-giver who authenticated the rules by virtue of his supreme power and whose will was known through the sacred books he directed human scribes to compose. This in turn meant that religious belief progressively lost its potency as a social cement; culture was no longer defined as a shared belief in the tenets of the Christian religion; and laws and principles were not validated automatically by reference to divine revelation. One instance of this secularizing trend can be found in the arguments marshalled against basing moral values wholly on religious assumptions developed by the philosopher John Stuart Mill. For example, in the second chapter of his book *On Liberty*, published in 1859, he wrote:

> I much fear that by attempting to form the mind and feelings on an exclusively religious type, and discarding those secular standards (as for want of a better name they may be called) which heretofore coexisted with and supplemented the Christian ethics... there will result, and is even now resulting, a low, abject, servile type of character, which, submit itself as it may to what it deems the Supreme Will, is incapable of rising to or sympathizing in the conception of Supreme Goodness. I believe that other ethics than any one which can be evolved from exclusively Christian sources, must exist side by side with Christian ethics to produce the moral regeneration of mankind; and that the Christian system is no exception to the rule that in an imperfect state of the human mind, the interests of truth require a diversity of opinions... It can do truth no service to blink the fact, known to all who have the most ordinary acquaintance with literary

history, that a large portion of the noblest and most valuable moral teaching has been the work, not only of men who did not know, but of men who knew and rejected, the Christian faith.

John Stuart Mill, the influential moral and political philosopher whose writings, including the book *On Liberty*, published in 1859, contributed to the growing 'secularization' of ideas about ethical and social values during Hopkins's lifetime.

Activity

What can you say about the attitude that Mill reveals in this passage to the link between religion and moral values?

Discussion

I sense that Mill is keen to lessen the significance attached to religion as the only source of values – his reference to *a low, abject, servile type of character* conveys his opinion of the sort of mind led to follow moral rules simply on the basis that they represent the word of God. At the same time Mill is not inclined to dismiss religious – specifically Christian – ideas altogether; terms like *co-existed* and *supplemented* suggest an apparently conciliatory tone. He makes reference to

Supreme Goodness and the *Supreme Will*, which might make us imagine he is identifying an all-powerful God as understood by theists – Jews, Muslims, Christians. But his final assertion that much of the finest thinking about morality has been done by men who actually rejected the Christian faith shows explicitly that his own affiliation is with *secular standards* – values based on human reasoning, not the revealed word of God – that often predate the beliefs introduced by theistic religion. I am left asking the question – 'Is Mill's *Supreme Will* at all like the God whom Christians believe created the world and revealed his plans for the human race in the Bible?'

This long-term process of attrition reached a critical watershed the same momentous year of 1859 – when Hopkins was a precocious adolescent winning prizes and standing up against authority at secondary school in north London – with the publication of Charles Darwin's *On the Origin of Species*. At this point the advance of secularism moves up several gears. From scrupulous study of the fossil records, complemented by first-hand investigation of the isolated fauna of the Galapagos Islands in the Pacific, Darwin concluded that all species – including human beings – were the result of natural selection over many millions of years. Subtle changes were constantly occurring in organisms; some worked, so the organism flourished and reproduced, passing inherited traits on to its descendants, while others didn't, so the organism perished. The key to the Darwinian explanation of nature was to be found in the randomness of this selection process – natural forms as we know them (including our own species) have evolved through a vast chain of chance modifications from progressively less 'adapted' versions as we travel back through the historical and pre-historical past. Humans do not merely resemble apes; we have evolved from them, we are their biological descendants. Which means, once and for all, that the literal account of creation offered by Christianity in the Book of Genesis is wholly inconsistent with a rational, scientific explanation of the evidence for the origins of life on earth.

This cartoon depicts a gorilla, offended by the connection that Darwin's *On the Origin of Species* makes between apes and human beings. The gorilla looks to the founder of the Society for the Prevention of Cruelty to Animals for support; he in turn addresses Darwin (on the right of the image) with the words, 'Now, Mr Darwin, how could you insult him so?' The image dates from 1871, just over a decade after the publication of Darwin's book. It is an example of the way middle-class society in Victorian Britain adapted ironic humour as its defence against uncomfortable new ideas.

One celebrated reflection on the spiritual void left by the increasing marginalization of belief is the poem *Dover Beach* by Matthew Arnold, first published in 1867 and almost certainly familiar to Hopkins, then a new convert to Roman Catholicism. The poem takes as its defining image the cold, impersonal sound of the waves breaking on a shingle beach at night. The poet associates the *grating roar* he hears with *the eternal note of sadness*, as he draws a parallel between his own regretful thoughts and those he attributes to the Greek tragic dramatist Sophocles, for whom the same endless rhythms evoked *the turbid ebb and flow/Of human misery.* If there is indeed no supreme being who created the universe and sustains it through his love, it follows that the values associated with belief are based on nothing more than a reassuring myth; religion has had its day, as the poet presents us with the comfortless and agnostic image of an ebbing tide destined never to return:

> The Sea of Faith
> Was once, too, at the full, and round earth's shore
> Lay like the folds of a bright girdle furl'd.
> But now I only hear
> Its melancholy, long, withdrawing roar,
> Retreating, to the breath
> Of the night-wind, down the vast edges drear
> And naked shingles of the world.

Activity

To what extent does the extract from Arnold's poem convey a sense of spiritual crisis?

Discussion

What is immediately striking is the pervasive sea/shore/tide imagery, and the subtle way Arnold invests it with spiritual weight. Faith is described in disturbing and catastrophic terms as a sea terminally ebbing – its vigour and life-sustaining qualities disappearing. One implication is that just as water is essential for creating and maintaining organic life on earth, so Faith has nourished spiritual life, providing purpose and comfort where it was otherwise absent. The fifth line acutely picks up the aural dimension, the rhythm dragging and heavily accentuated, the vowels long and strung out, evocative of something grimly final – the world, seemingly now empty of purpose, is *drear*, its landscape the sterile and comfortless vista of *naked shingles*. Unlike Mill or Darwin, Arnold finds nothing to celebrate in human reason, in the advance of the secular world; the poem rather hints at a mixture of grief and anxiety as the poet contemplates the emptiness of a universe rendered Godless.

A portrait of the poet, essayist (and school inspector) Matthew Arnold. His poem *Dover Beach* famously articulates some of the acute spiritual concerns felt by those who saw the human and cultural value of religious belief but were finding it progressively harder to justify such belief in terms of reason and evidence.

What has this to do with Hopkins and his poetry? Both his life and his writing can be seen as standing against some of the main currents of contemporary cultural developments. He is a heterodox (non-conforming) figure, although it is important to say that this alone does not mean he is wrong (or indeed right) in his beliefs. The fact that his poetry embodies a set of very specific religious beliefs that others found increasingly hard to reconcile with their understanding of the natural world, does not make that poetry special in any way. What matters is the intrinsic quality of the verse.

But there are other aspects of the *Zeitgeist* – the 'spirit of the age' – where he is more in tune with contemporary feeling. To appreciate this, we need to look at some of his formative experiences as an undergraduate at Balliol College, Oxford, between 1863 and 1867. Hopkins was a very able student (he achieved first-class honours) but Oxford was even more significant for him spiritually than academically. While there, he converted from Anglicanism to Roman Catholicism. This involved him in much soul-searching – he knew it was something he had to do, but he was also sensitive to the distress it would cause his family. Why did he convert? He was brought up in a 'high' Anglican environment – the ritual and iconography of that expression of religious belief had a great deal in common with Roman Catholicism. What most fundamentally distinguished the two expressions of belief however was the Catholic doctrine of 'the real presence'; the bread and wine used in the communion service *became* at the Offertory, through the agency of the priest performing the ritual, the body and blood of Christ. This belief in 'transubstantiation' was the defining aspect of Catholic doctrine that non-Catholic Christians found hardest to accept. By contrast, writing to a school and college contemporary in 1864, aged 20 – two years before his actual conversion – Hopkins asserted confidently that:

The great aid to belief and object of belief is the doctrine of the Real Presence in the Blessed Sacrament of the Altar. Religion without that is sombre, dangerous, illogical, with that it is – not to speak of its grand consistency and certainty – *loveable*. Hold that and you will gain all Catholic truth.

So, two polarized aspects of context for Hopkins's poetry – secularism and the decline in the centrality of religious belief on the one hand, a very traditional and ritualistic version of Christian faith and practice on the other.

A third element in the contextual map is provided by the movement known as 'aestheticism'. This movement was famously encapsulated in the formula 'Art for Art's sake', and it rejected the notion that art should have a social or moral purpose. Aestheticism was associated with a renewed critical interest in the visual art of the classical world and the Renaissance (the movement during the fourteenth to the sixteenth centuries which revitalized interest in classical art and literature). It can at least in part be characterized as an attempt to ascribe to great works of art the transcendent importance formerly given to the divine revelation experienced by religious believers. One of the key figures in this development was the Oxford scholar Walter Pater, a few years older than Hopkins and for a time one of his tutors at Oxford. It was Pater in the conclusion to his influential work *The Renaissance* who declared that:

Art comes to you proposing frankly to give nothing but the highest quality to your moments as they pass and simply for those moments' sake.

The aesthetic movement constituted a 'religion of beauty' to the extent that it regarded great art as having permanent significance in a world where all other experience was mundane and conditional. It was art that gave life whatever value or meaning it might possess – so to that extent it could be seen as having a religious function. It is also important to appreciate that aestheticism is in large measure a reaction to the increasing materialism of life in the latter half of the nineteenth century, to the loss of 'spiritual' values evidenced in the decline of religious belief as well as to the unprecedented ugliness and misery associated with the processes of industrialization.

As a great centre of scholarship, with a wealth of fine medieval architecture, Oxford was largely protected from the factories and their associated working-class slum dwellings that disfigured many towns in the nineteenth century. It was an apt location for a writer such as Pater with his cult of the beautiful. And it is significant that Hopkins found Oxford congenial in terms of the physical as well as the social and intellectual environment. His own letters and Journal entries at this period confirm in particular his extraordinary sensitivity to the aesthetic in nature. He had some practical facility in painting and sketching (as well as aspirations later in life to musical composition), and at least two of his younger brothers went on to earn their livings as artists and illustrators. It seems entirely fitting that he should find himself at Oxford in the early years of the aesthetic movement – art as a way of apprehending and conveying beauty was in his blood.

This is a mid-nineteenth century print of Oxford by Akerman. For Hopkins, Oxford played a hugely significant role in his spiritual, intellectual and imaginative development. In the poem *Duns Scotus's Oxford* he praises an idealized image set in a medieval past – *towery city and branchy between towers* – while recognizing the contemporary beginnings of urban sprawl at its edges, a phenomenon he dismisses as *graceless growth*.

Oxford was of practical importance in Hopkins's development for yet another reason. His decision to convert to Roman Catholicism was by no means unique; other young men of his generation, usually sharing his high Anglican background, agonized in similar fashion over the spiritual direction they ought to follow. It was an internal drama first rehearsed two decades earlier by the hugely influential figure of John Henry Newman, when he finally became a Catholic in 1845.

This was an event that sent shockwaves through the Anglican Communion, since Newman had been identified in the so-called 'Oxford Movement' since the 1830s with efforts within Anglicanism to re-discover the purity of the early Christian church. It is therefore both significant and unsurprising that it was to Newman that Hopkins wrote about his conversion plans, that it was Newman himself who received him into the Catholic church. It was as a teacher at Newman's Oratory School in Birmingham that Hopkins spent his first working months as a Catholic – and arguably, from the evidence of his letters, where he first experienced the low spirits brought on by nervous exhaustion that seem to have characterized much of his subsequent life as a teacher and priest.

The internal context

There is no suggestion in Hopkins's work of the kind of profound agnostic doubts identified in Arnold's *Dover Beach*. While you will see that his poems do convey spiritual anxiety and doubt, it is generally in the context of Hopkins's depressed perception of himself as unworthy of God's love or care. Hopkins can powerfully articulate a real sense of estrangement from the divine in his poems, and that sense can excite in him feelings of despair and grief, but nowhere does he suggest doubt about God's existence or an inscrutable divine providence that sustains the universe.

Less than two years after his conversion (October 1866), Hopkins began the lengthy course of study and reflection that would eventually lead to his ordination as a Jesuit priest. The critical elements in any consideration of Hopkins's 'internal context' are his profound awareness of beauty, his sense of himself and the elusive nature of human consciousness – and the links that can be made between these and the priestly vocation, especially as mediated by the spirituality of the Society of Jesus.

The hypothesis pursued here identifies his decision to become a priest as involving both positive and negative factors. Chief among the positives would be his undoubted sense of a vocation, a calling to serve God's will through a priestly ministry. That the priesthood offered a robust structure for serving God at the cost of personal convenience, involving both self-denial and total submission to the dictates of his superiors, only enhanced the attraction of the choice in Hopkins's mind. The letters and Journals, as well as testimony from those who knew him, provide ample evidence of Hopkins's life-long tendency to 'ascesis' – mastering the will through mortification of various kinds – as a means of better serving God and resisting the temptations of evil. But it is also therefore possible to see the decision to become a priest as a choice with a negative aspect; was Hopkins consciously or otherwise seeking an escape from the snares of worldly pleasure in submitting himself to the quasi-military discipline of the Jesuits?

There is a revealing comment in a letter composed when Hopkins was teaching at Newman's school (February 1868). Having written of his priestly calling that *Besides that it is the happiest and best way, it is the only one*, he reminds his correspondent that he had once had artistic ambitions but continues:

Even if I could I wd. not I think, now, for the fact is that the higher and more attractive parts of the art put a strain upon the passions which I shd. think it unsafe to encounter.

Just as temporal armies have their drills aimed at instilling discipline and order, so the Jesuits had a close spiritual parallel: the *Spiritual Exercises* devised by the order's sixteenth-century Spanish founder, St Ignatius Loyola. These exercises became known as the Ignatian Exercises. In this work Ignatius used various dramatic and imaginative prompts to make the individual's meditation on the meaning of the life of Jesus as intense and 'felt' as possible. Remember that the Jesuits were the 'shock troops' of the Catholic church in what is known as the

Counter-Reformation, that period in the sixteenth and seventeenth centuries when Catholicism was engaging in theological debate with the ideas of the Protestant 'reformers'. To be a Jesuit was to be identified as an intellectually combative, resilient and quick-witted priest, sent by your superiors to whatever war zone was considered most suitable for your particular skills and aptitudes. But it is also important to remember that the Jesuits' mission was spiritual and that to execute it effectively they required the kind of renewal of their own spiritual energies that the Ignatian Exercises were meant to promote.

Hopkins had a deep affinity for this material. One of his prose works, *Comments on the Spiritual Exercises of St Ignatius Loyola*, offers some valuable clues as to what he found most compelling when he reflected on the great religious theme of creation – the core belief, common to devout Jews, Muslims and Christians, that God created the world from nothing, and in creating it gave special status to humankind as 'made in His image' (Genesis 1:27). Hopkins's reflections are fascinating because they provide a key to some of the most deep-seated themes in his poetry – to that extent perhaps its most important 'context' can be found in the ideas expressed in these *Comments*. Hopkins exercises his imagination – as encouraged by Ignatius over 250 years earlier – to reflect on the unique quality of his own consciousness as the thing through which he comprehends God's creation, and he does so as only a poet could, using supercharged and deeply sensuous language in one of the most remarkable passages in the whole of Victorian literature:

> When I consider my selfbeing, my consciousness and feeling of myself, that taste of myself, *of I* and *me* above and in all things, which is more distinctive than the taste of ale or alum, more distinctive than the smell of walnutleaf or camphor, and is incommunicable by any means to another man (as when I was a child I used to ask myself: What must it be to be someone else?). Nothing else in nature comes near this unspeakable stress

**of pitch, distinctiveness, and selving, this selfbeing of my own...
searching nature I taste *self* but at one tankard, that of my own
being.**

Central here is the notion of 'selving', the unique quality that
differentiates one thing from another. In the case of humans, that
one thing is self-consciousness, the incommunicable awareness of
an inner life, the existence of mind. The term most used by
Hopkins to denote his sense of the inner 'self' of everything
observed in the natural world is **inscape**; the term, and its link to
the poetry, is explored in more detail in the Interpretations
section later in this book. For now, all you need to appreciate is
that this concept was the fundamental building-block in
Hopkins's sense of the world and himself. He read the medieval
philosopher Duns Scotus, found in his writing the (Latin) term
Haecceitas ('thisness') and realized that at least one other thinker
in history was as excited as he was himself by the individual, the
specific, rather than by the universal or general. The coinage
'inscape' denotes the concealed key unique to everything in
nature that can be unlocked in a moment of heightened
perception. It makes sense to see much of the energy released in
the poems as Hopkins's attempt to replicate the 'inscape' of a
perception through a uniquely charged arrangement of words
and rhythms.

In summary, there were currents in the contemporary world
that accorded with Hopkins's own sense of the value of beauty
– the ideas of Walter Pater, for instance – just as in John Henry
Newman there was the role model of the Anglican intellectual
and priest who finds his spiritual home in the Roman Catholic
church. But other currents were less sympathetic. The growing
secularism of the Victorian era was alien to Hopkins's
profoundly religious sensibility, while his letters and journal
entries variously evoked his revulsion and sadness at the
sordidness of a social and economic order where the urban
masses were mere cogs in a vast machine. His pastoral work in
Lancashire parishes between 1879 and 1881 gave him first-hand

experience of the human cost of capitalism. Fuelling this secularism was a science that challenged the orthodox Christian explanation of the world, embodied most iconically in the person of Darwin. Arnold's poem *Dover Beach* was only one of many literary expressions of the troubled agnosticism that scientific thinking increasingly provoked.

In terms of Hopkins's own mind, the chief informing factors were Catholic thinkers from distant times: St Ignatius Loyola for the meditative structure his writings encouraged Hopkins to adopt in his own imaginative response to the world, and Duns Scotus for showing Hopkins the strong philosophical case for regarding particular things – individual trees, clouds, birds or people – as each having its own unique essence that we can experience through a direct intuition. In finding Jesuit spirituality so congenial, as in discovering a philosophical kindred spirit from the Middle Ages, it is clear that Hopkins was in many respects a reactionary figure, in opposition to much of the prevailing 'spirit of the age'. But you will find in his poems some of the most exciting, complex and innovative ideas and techniques in the whole of Victorian literature. The most important link between Hopkins the poet and his 'contexts' may be this: whatever contemporary science implied about nature being a set of complex physical processes that did not need the hypothesis of a divine being, Hopkins achieved a body of work that is unintelligible without the concept of a God who informs everything in nature, who is to be loved but also feared. We as readers do not need to share Hopkins's absolute belief in the living reality of that figure, but we do need to recognize that this is the ultimate context within which his poems find their meaning and purpose.

The Poems

Heaven-Haven
(*a nun takes the veil*)

> I have desired to go
>> Where springs not fail,
> To fields where flies no sharp and sided hail
>> And a few lilies blow.
>
> And I have asked to be
>> Where no storms come,
> Where the green swell is in the havens dumb,
>> And out of the swing of the sea.

The Habit of Perfection

Elected Silence, sing to me
And beat upon my whorlèd ear,
Pipe me to pastures still and be
The music that I care to hear.

Shape nothing, lips; be lovely-dumb:
It is the shut, the curfew sent
From there where all surrenders come
Which only makes you eloquent.

Be shellèd, eyes, with double dark
10 And find the uncreated light:
This ruck and reel which you remark
Coils, keeps, and teases simple sight.

Palate, the hutch of tasty lust,
Desire not to be rinsed with wine:
The can must be so sweet, the crust
So fresh that come in fasts divine!

Nostrils, your careless breath that spend
Upon the stir and keep of pride,
What relish shall the censers send
20 Along the sanctuary side!

O feel-of-primrose hands, O feet
That want the yield of plushy sward,
But you shall walk the golden street
And you unhouse and house the Lord.

And, Poverty, be thou the bride
And now the marriage feast begun,
And lily-coloured clothes provide
Your spouse not laboured-at nor spun.

The Wreck of the Deutschland

Dec. 6, 7 1875

to the happy memory of five Franciscan nuns, exiles by the
Falck Laws, drowned between midnight and morning of
December 7.

Part the first
Thou mastering me
God! giver of breath and bread;
World's strand, sway of the sea;
Lord of living and dead;
Thou hast bound bones and veins in me, fastened
me flesh,
And after it álmost únmade, what with dread,
Thy doing: and dost thou touch me afresh?
Over again I feel thy finger and find theé.

II
I did say yes
O at lightning and lashed rod;
Thou heardst me truer than tongue confess
Thy terror, O Christ, O God;
Thou knowest the walls, altar and hour and night:
The swoon of a heart that the sweep and the hurl of
thee trod
Hard down with a horror of height:
And the midriff astrain with leaning of, laced with fire of
stress.

10

III

The frown of his face
Before me, the hurtle of hell
Behind, where, where was a, where was a place?
20   I whirled out wings that spell
And fled with a fling of the heart to the heart of the
Host.
My heart, but you were dovewinged, I can tell,
Carrier-witted, I am bold to boast,
To flash from the flame to the flame then, tower from the
grace to the grace.

IV

I am sóft síft
In an hourglass — at the wall
Fast, but mined with a motion, a drift,
And it crowds and it combs to the fall;
I steady as a water in a well, to a poise, to a pane,
30   But roped with, always, all the way down from the
tall
Fells or flanks of the voel, a vein
Of the gospel proffer, a pressure, a principle, Christ's gift.

V

I kiss my hand
To the stars, lovely-asunder
Starlight, wafting him out of it; and
Glow, glory in thunder;
Kiss my hand to the dappled-with-damson west:
Since, though he is under the world's splendour and
wonder,
His mystery must be instressed, stressed;
40   For I greet him the days I meet him, and bless when I
understand.

VI

Not out of his bliss
Springs the stress felt
Nor first from heaven (and few know this)
Swings the stroke dealt –
Stroke and a stress that stars and storms deliver,
That guilt is hushed by, hearts are flushed by and
melt –
But it rides time like riding a river
(And here the faithful waver, the faithless fable and
miss.)

VII

It dates from day
Of his going in Galilee;
Warm-laid grave of a womb-life grey;
Manger, maiden's knee;
The dense and the driven Passion, and frightful
sweat;
Thence the discharge of it, there its swelling to be,
Though felt before, though in high flood yet –
What none would have known of it, only the heart, being
hard at bay,

VIII

Is out with it! Oh,
We lash with the best or worst
Word last! How a lush-kept plush-capped sloe
Will, mouthed to flesh-burst,
Gush! – flush the man, the being with it, sour or
sweet,
Brim, in a flash, full! – Hither then, last or first,
To hero of Calvary, Christ's feet –
Never ask if meaning it, wanting it, warned of it – men go.

IX

Be adored among men,
God, three-numberèd form;
Wring thy rebel, dogged in den,
Man's malice, with wrecking and storm.
Beyond saying sweet, past telling of tongue,
70 Thou art lightning and love, I found it, a winter and
warm;
Father and fondler of heart thou hast wrung;
Hast thy dark descending and most art merciful then.

X

With an anvil-ding
And with fire in him forge thy will
Or rather, rather then, stealing as Spring
Through him, melt him but master him still:
Whether át ónce, as once at a crash Paul,
Or as Austin, a lingering-out sweet skill,
Make mercy in all of us, out of us all
80 Mastery, but be adored, but be adored King.

Part the second

XI

'Some find me a sword; some
The flange and the rail; flame,
Fang, or flood' goes Death on drum,
And storms bugle his fame.
But wé dréam we are rooted in earth – Dust!
Flesh falls within sight of us, we, though our flower the
same,
Wave with the meadow, forget that there must
The sour scythe cringe, and the blear share come.

XII

On Saturday sailed from Bremen,
90   American-outward-bound,
Take settler and seamen, tell men with women,
Two hundred souls in the round –
O Father, not under thy feathers nor ever as guessing
The goal was a shoal, of a fourth the doom to be
drowned;
Yet díd the dark side of the bay of thy blessing
Not vault them, the million of rounds of thy mercy not reeve
even them in?

XIII

Into the snows she sweeps,
Hurling the haven behind,
The Deutschland, on Sunday; and so the sky keeps,
100   For the infinite air is unkind,
And the sea flint-flake, black-backed in the regular blow,
Sitting Eastnortheast, in cursed quarter, the wind;
Wiry and white-fiery and whírlwind-swivellèd
snow
Spins to the widow-making unchilding unfathering deeps.

XIV

She drove in the dark to leeward,
She struck – not a reef or a rock
But the combs of a smother of sand: night drew her
Dead to the Kentish Knock;
And she beat the bank down with her bows and the ride
of her keel;
110   The breakers rolled on her beam with ruinous shock;
And canvass and compass, the whorl and the wheel
Idle for ever to waft her or wind her with, these she endured.

XV

Hope had grown grey hairs,
Hope had mourning on,
Trenched with tears, carved with cares,
Hope was twelve hours gone;
And frightful a nightfall folded rueful a day
Nor rescue, only rocket and lightship, shone,
And lives at last were washing away:
120 To the shrouds they took, – they shook in the hurling and
horrible airs.

XVI

One stirred from the rigging to save
The wild woman-kind below,
With a rope's end round the man, handy and
brave –
He was pitched to his death at a blow,
For all his dreadnought breast and braids of thew:
They could tell him for hours, dandled the to and fro
Through the cobbled foam-fleece. What could he do
With the burl of the fountains of air, buck and the flood of the
wave?

XVII

They fought with God's cold –
130 And they could not and fell to the deck
(Crushed them) or water (and drowned them) or
rolled
With the sea-romp over the wreck.
Night roared, with the heart-break hearing a heart-broke
rabble,
The woman's wailing, the crying of child without
check –
Till a lioness arose breasting the babble,
A prophetess towered in the tumult, a virginal tongue told.

XVIII

Ah, touched in your bower of bone
Are you! turned for an exquisite smart,
Have you! make words break from me here all
alone,
140   Do you! – mother of being in me, heart.
O unteachably after evil, but uttering truth,
Why, tears! is it? tears; such a melting, a madriga
start!
Never-eldering revel and river of youth,
What can it be, this glee? the good you have there of your
own?

XIX

Sister, a sister calling
A master, her master and mine! –
And the inboard seas run swirling and hawling;
The rash smart sloggering brine
Blinds her; but shé that weather sees óne thing, one;
150   Has óne fetch ín her: she rears herself to divine
Ears, and the call of the tall nun
To the men in the tops and the tackle rode over the
storm's brawling.

XX

She was first of a five and came
Of a coifèd sisterhood.
(O Deutschland, double a desperate name!
O world wide of its good!
But Gertrude, lily, and Luther, are two of a town,
Christ's lily and beast of the waste wood:
From life's dawn it is drawn down,
160   Abel is Cain's brother and breasts they have sucked the
same.)

XXI

Loathed for a love men knew in them,
Banned by the land of their birth,
Rhine refused them, Thames would ruin them;
Surf, snow, river and earth
Gnashed: but thou art above, thou Orion of light;
Thy unchancelling poising palms were weighing the
worth,
Thou martyr-master: in thý sight
Storm flakes were scroll-leaved flowers, lily showers – sweet
heaven was astrew in them.

XXII

Five! the finding and sake
And cipher of suffering Christ.
Mark, the mark is of man's make
And the word of it Sacrificed.
But he scores it in scarlet himself on his own
bespoken,
Before-time-taken, dearest prizèd and priced –
Stigma, signal, cinquefoil token
For lettering of the lamb's fleece, ruddying of the rose-flake.

XXIII

Joy fall to thee, father Francis,
Drawn to the Life that died;
With the gnarls of the nails in thee, niche of the
lance, his
Lovescape crucified
And seal of his seraph-arrival! and these thy
daughters
And five-livèd and leavèd favour and pride,
Are sisterly sealed in wild waters,
To bathe in his fall-gold mercies, to breathe in his all-fire
glances.

170

180

XXIV

Away in the loveable west,
On a pastoral forehead of Wales,
I was under a roof here, I was at rest,
And they the prey of the gales;
She to the black-about air, to the breaker, the thickly
190   Falling flakes, to the throng that catches and quails
Was calling 'O Christ, Christ, come quickly':
The cross to her she calls Christ to her, christens her wild-
worst Best.

XXV

The majesty! what did she mean?
Breathe, arch and original Breath.
Is it lóve in her of the béing as her lóver had
béen?
Breathe, body of lovely Death.
They were else-minded then, altogether, the men
Wóke thee with a *We are périshing* in the wéather of
Gennésaréth.
Or ís it that she cried for the crown then,
200   The keener to come at the comfort for feeling the
combating keen?

XXVI

For how to the heart's cheering
The down-dugged ground-hugged grey
Hovers off, the jay-blue heavens appearing
Of pied and peeled May!
Blue-beating and hoary-glow height; or night, still
higher,
With belled fire and the moth-soft Milky Way,
What by your measure is the heaven of desire,
The treasure never eyesight got, nor was ever guessed what
for the hearing?

XXVII

Nó, but it was nót these.
The jading and jar of the cart,
Time's tásking, it is fathers that asking for ease
Of the sodden-with-its sorrowing heart,
Not danger, electrical horror; then further it finds
The appealing of the Passion is tenderer in prayer
apart:
Other, I gather, in measure her mind's
Burden, in wind's burly and beat of endragonèd seas.

XXVIII

But how shall I... make me room there:
Reach me a... Fancy, come faster –
Strike you the sight of it? look at it loom there,
Thing that she... There then! the Master,
Ipse, the only one, Christ, King, Head:
He was to cure the extremity where he had cast her;
Do, deal, lord it with living and dead;
Let him ride, her pride, in his triumph, despatch and have
done with his doom there.

XXIX

Ah! there was a heart right!
There was single eye!
Read the unshapeable shock night
And knew the who and the why;
Wording it how but by him that present and past,
Heaven and earth are word of, worded by? –
The Simon Peter of a soul! to the blast
Tárpéïan-fast, but a blown beacon of light.

XXX

Jesu, heart's light,
Jesu, maid's son,
What was the feast followed the night
Thou hadst glory of this nun? –
Féast of the óne wóman withóut stáin.
For so conceivèd, so to conceive thee is done;
But here was heart-throe, birth of a brain,
Word, that heard and kept thee and uttered thee óutríght.

XXXI

Well, shé has thée for the pain, for the
Patience; but pity of the rest of them!
Heart, go and bleed at a bitterer vein for the
Comfortless unconfessed of them –
No not uncomforted: lovely-felicitous Providence
Fínger of a ténder of, O of a féathery délicacy, the bréast
of the
Maiden could obey so, be a bell to, ring óf it, and
Startle the poor sheep back! is the shipwrack then a harvest,
does tempest carry the grain for thee?

XXXII

I admire thee, master of the tides,
Of the Yore-flood, of the year's fall;
The recurb and the recovery of the gulf's sides,
The girth of it and the wharf of it and the wall;
Stanching, quenching ocean of a motionable mind;
Ground of being, and granite of it: pást áll
Grásp Gód, thróned behínd
Death with a sovereignty that heeds but hides, bodes but
abides;

240

250

XXXIII

With a mercy that outrides
The all of water, an ark
For the listener; for the lingerer with a love glides
Lower than death and the dark;
A vein for the visiting of the past-prayer, pent in prison,
The-last-breath penitent spirits – the uttermost mark
Our passion-plungèd giant risen,
The Christ of the Father compassionate, fetched in the storm
of his strides.

XXXIV

Now burn, new born to the world,
Double-naturèd name,
The heaven-flung, heart-fleshed, maiden-furled
Miracle-in-Mary-of-flame,
Mid-numberèd he in three of the thunder-throne!
Not a dooms-day dazzle in his coming nor dark as he
came;
Kind, but royally reclaiming his own;
A released shówer, let flásh to the shíre, not a líghtning of fíre
hard-húrled.

XXXV

Dame, at our door
Drówned, and among oúr shóals,
Remember us in the roads, the heaven-haven of the
reward:
Our Kíng back, Oh, upon Énglish sóuls!
Let him easter in us, be a dayspring to the dimness of us,
be a crimson-cresseted east,
More brightening her, rare-dear Britain, as his reign rolls,
Pride, rose, prince, hero of us, high-priest,
Our héarts' charity's héarth's fíre, our thóughts' chivalry's
thróng's Lórd.

Moonrise

I awoke in the midsummer not-to-call night, | in the
    white and the walk of the morning:
The móon, dwíndled and thínned to the frínge | of a
    fíngernail héld to the cándle,
Or páring of páradisáïcal frúit, | lóvely in wáning but
    lústreless,
Stepped from the stool, drew back from the barrow, | of
    dark Maenefa the mountain;
A cusp still clasped him, a fluke yet fanged him, |
    entangled him, not quit utterly.
This was the prized, the desirable sight, | unsought,
    presented so easily,
Parted me leaf and leaf, divided me, | eyelid and eyelid
    of slumber.

God's Grandeur

The world is charged with the grandeur of God.
    It will flame out, like shining from shook foil;
    It gathers to a greatness, like the ooze of oil
Crushed. Why do men then now not reck his rod?
Generations have trod, have trod, have trod;
    And all is seared with trade; bleared, smeared with toil;
    And wears man's smudge and shares man's smell: the soil
Is bare now, nor can foot feel, being shod.

And, for all this, nature is never spent;
    There lives the dearest freshness deep down things;
And though the last lights off the black West went
    Oh, morning, at the brown brink eastwards, springs –
Because the Holy Ghost over the bent
    World broods with warm breast and with ah! bright wings.

The Starlight Night

Look at the stars! look, look up at the skies!
    O look at all the fire-folk sitting in the air!
    The bright boroughs, the circle-citadels there!
Down in dim woods the diamond delves! the elves'-eyes!
The grey lawns cold where gold, where quickgold lies!
    Wind-beat whitebeam! airy abeles set on a flare!
    Flake-doves sent floating forth at a farmyard scare! –
Ah well! it is all a purchase, all is a prize.

Buy then! bid then! – What? – Prayer, patience, alms, vows.
Look, look: a May-mess, like on orchard boughs!
    Look! March-bloom, like on mealed-with-yellow sallows!
These are indeed the barn; withindoors house
The shocks. This piece-bright paling shuts the spouse
    Christ home, Christ and his mother and all his hallows.

31

'As kingfishers catch fire'

As kingfishers catch fire, dragonflies draw flame;
    As tumbled over rim in roundy wells
    Stones ring; like each tucked string tells, each hung bell's
Bow swung finds tongue to fling out broad its name;
Each mortal thing does one thing and the same:
    Deals out that being indoors each one dwells;
    Selves – goes its self; *myself* it speaks and spells,
Crying *What I do is me: for that I came.*

I say more: the just man justices;
    Keeps grace: that keeps all his goings graces;
Acts in God's eye what in God's eye he is –
    Christ. For Christ plays in ten thousand places,
Lovely in limbs, and lovely in eyes not his
    To the Father through the features of men's faces.

Spring

Nothing is so beautiful as Spring –
    When weeds, in wheels, shoot long and lovely and lush;
    Thrush's eggs look little low heavens, and thrush
Through the echoing timber does so rinse and wring

The ear, it strikes like lightnings to hear him sing;
    The glassy peartree leaves and blooms, they brush
    The descending blue; that blue is all in a rush
With richness; the racing lambs too have fair their fling.

What is all this juice and all this joy?
    A strain of the earth's sweet being in the beginning
In Eden garden. – Have, get before it cloy,

    Before it cloud, Christ, lord, and sour with sinning,
Innocent mind and Mayday in girl and boy,
    Most, O maid's child, thy choice and worthy the winning.

The Sea and the Skylark

On ear and ear two noises too old to end
    Trench – right, the tide that ramps against the shore;
    With a flood or a fall, low lull-off or all roar,
Frequenting there while moon shall wear and wend.

Left hand, off land, I hear the lark ascend,
    His rash-fresh re-winded new-skeinèd score
    In crisps of curl off wild winch whirl, and pour
And pelt music, till none's to spill nor spend.

How these two shame this shallow and frail town!
10   How ring right out our sordid turbid time,
Being pure! We, life's pride and cared-for crown,

    Have lost that cheer and charm of earth's past prime:
Our make and making break, are breaking, down
    To man's last dust, drain fast towards man's first slime.

In the Valley of the Elwy

I remember a house where all were good
    To me, God knows, deserving no such thing:
    Comforting smell breathed at very entering,
Fetched fresh, as I suppose, off some sweet wood.

That cordial air made those kind people a hood
    All over, as a bevy of eggs the mothering wing
    Will, or mild nights the new morsels of Spring:
Why, it séemed of coúrse; séemed of ríght it shóuld.

Lovely the woods, waters, meadows, combes, vales,
10 All the air things wear that build this world of Wales;
    Only the inmate does not correspond:

God, lover of souls, swaying considerate scales,
Complete thy creature dear O where it fails,
    Being mighty a master, being a father and fond.

33

The Windhover:
to Christ our Lord

I caught this morning morning's minion, king-
  dom of daylight's dauphin, dapple-dáwn-drawn Falcon, in
   his riding
  Of the rólling level úndernéath him steady áir, and stríding
High there, how he rung upon the rein of a wimpling wing
In his ecstacy! then off, off forth on swing,
  As a skate's heel sweeps smooth on a bow-bend: the hurl
   and gliding
  Rebuffed the big wind. My heart in hiding
Stirred for a bird, – the achieve of, the mastery of the thing!

Brute beauty and valour and act, oh, air, pride, plume, here
10 Buckle! AND the fire that breaks from thee then, a billion
Times told lovelier, more dangerous, O my chevalier!

  No wónder of it: shéer plód makes plóugh down síllion
Shine, and blue-bleak embers, ah my dear,
  Fall, gáll themsélves, and gásh góld-vermílion.

Pied Beauty

Glory be to God for dappled things –
    For skies of couple-colour as a brinded cow;
        For rose-moles all in stipple upon trout that swim;
Fresh-firecoal chestnut-falls; finches' wings;
    Landscape plotted and pieced – fold, fallow, and plough;
        And áll trades, their gear and tackle and trim.

All things counter, original, spáre, strange;
    Whatever is fickle, frecklèd (who knows how?)
        With swíft, slów; sweet, sóur; adázzle, dím;
10 He fathers-forth whose beauty is pást change:
                Práise hím.

The Caged Skylark

As a dare-gale skylark scanted in a dull cage,
    Man's mounting spirit in his bone-house, mean house,
      dwells –
    That bird beyond the remembering hís free fells;
This in drudgery, day-labouring-out life's age.

Though aloft on turf or perch or poor low stage
    Both sing sometímes the sweetest, sweetest spells,
    Yet both droop deadly sómetimes in their cells
Or wring their barriers in bursts of fear or rage.

Not that the sweet-fowl, song-fowl, needs no rest –
10 Why, hear him, hear him babble and drop down to his nest,
    But his own nest, wild nest, no prison.

Man's spirit will be flesh-bound, when found at best,
But úncúmberèd: meadow-dówn is nót distréssed
    For a ráinbow fóoting it nor hé for his bónes rísen.

Hurrahing in Harvest

Summer ends now; now, barbarous in beauty, the stooks
    rise
Around; up above, what wind-walks! what lovely
    behaviour
Of silk-sack clouds! has wilder, wilful-wavier
Meal-drift moulded ever and melted across skies?

I wálk, I líft up, Í lift úp heart, éyes,
Down all that glory in the heavens to glean our Saviour;
And, éyes, héart, what looks, what lips yet gáve you a
Rapturous love's greeting of realer, of rounder replies?

And the azurous hung hills are his world-wielding shoulder
10   Majestic – as a stallion stalwart, very-violet-sweet! –
These things, these things were here and but the beholder
Wánting; whích two whén they ónce méet,
The heart rears wings bold and bolder
And hurls for him, O half hurls earth for him off under
    his feet.

The Loss of the Eurydice
foundered March 24 1878

The Eurydice – it concerned thee, O Lord:
Three hundred souls, O alas! on board,
    Some asleep unawakened, all un-
Warned, eleven fathoms fallen

Where she foundered! One stroke
Felled and furled them, the hearts of oak!
    And flockbells off the aerial
Downs' forefalls beat to the burial.

For did she pride her, freighted fully, on
10 Bounden bales or a hoard of bullion? –
    Precious passing measure,
Lads and men her lade and treasure.

She had come from a cruise, training seamen –
Men, boldboys soon to be men:
    Must it, worst weather,
Blast bole and bloom together?

No Atlantic squall overwrought her
Or rearing billow of the Biscay water:
    Home was hard at hand
20 And the blow bore from land.

And you were a liar, O blue March day.
Bright sun lanced fire in the heavenly bay;
    But what black Boreas wrecked her? he
Came equipped, deadly-electric,

A beetling baldbright cloud thorough England
Riding: there did storms not mingle? and
    Hailropes hustle and grind their
Heavengravel? wolfsnow, worlds of it, wind there?

Now Carisbrook keep goes under in gloom;
30   Now it overvaults Appledurcombe;
        Now near by Ventnor town
It hurls, hurls off Boniface Down.

Too proud, too proud, what a press she bore!
Royal, and all her royals wore.
        Sharp with her, shorten sail!
Too late; lost; gone with the gale.

This was that fell capsize.
As half she had righted and hoped to rise
        Death teeming in by her portholes
40   Raced down decks, round messes of mortals.

Then a lurch forward, frigate and men;
'All hands for themselves' the cry ran then;
        But she who had housed them thither
Was around them, bound them or wound them with her.

Marcus Hare, high her captain,
Kept to her – care-drowned and wrapped in
        Cheer's death, would follow
His charge through the champ-white water-in-a-wallow,

All under Channel to bury in a beach her
50   Cheeks: Right, rude of feature,
        He thought he heard say
'Her commander! and thou too, and thou this way.'

It is even seen, time's something server,
In mankind's medley a duty-swerver,
        At downright 'No or Yes?'
Doffs all, drives full for righteousness.

Sydney Fletcher, Bristol-bred,
(Low lie his mates now on watery bed)
        Takes to the seas and snows
60   As sheer down the ship goes.

Now her afterdraught gullies him too down;
Now he wrings for breath with the deathgush brown;
    Till a lifebelt and God's will
Lend him a lift from the sea-swill.

Now he shoots short up to the round air;
Now he gasps, now he gazes everywhere;
    But his eye no cliff, no coast or
Mark makes in the rivelling snowstorm.

Him, after an hour of wintry waves,
70 A schooner sights, with another, and saves,
    And he boards her in Oh! such joy
He has lost count what came next, poor boy. –

They say who saw one sea-corpse cold
He was all of lovely manly mould,
    Every inch a tar,
Of the best we boast our sailors are.

Look, foot to forelock, how all things suit! he
Is strung by duty, is strained to beauty,
    And brown-as-dawning-skinned
80 With brine and shine and whirling wind.

O his nimble finger, his gnarled grip!
Leagues, leagues of seamanship
    Slumber in these forsaken
Bones, this sinew, and will not waken.

He was but one like thousands more.
Day and night I deplore
    My people and born own nation,
Fast foundering own generation.

I might let bygones be – our curse
90 Of ruinous shrine no hand or, worse,
    Robbery's hand is busy to
Dress, hoar-hallowèd shrines unvisited;

Only the breathing temple and fleet
Life, this wildworth blown so sweet,
    These daredeaths, ay this crew, in
Unchrist, all rolled in ruin –

Deeply surely I need to deplore it,
Wondering why my master bore it,
    The riving off that race
100 So at home, time was, to his truth and grace

That a starlight-wender of ours would say
The marvellous Milk was Walsingham Way
    And one – but let be, let be:
More, more than was will yet be. –

O well wept, mother have lost son;
Wept, wife; wept, sweetheart would be one:
    Though grief yield them no good
Yet shed what tears sad truelove should.

But to Christ lord of thunder
110 Crouch; lay knee by earth low under:
    'Holiest, loveliest, bravest,
Save my hero, O Hero savest.

And the prayer thou hearst me making
Have, at the awful overtaking,
    Heard; have heard and granted
Grace that day grace was wanted.'

Not that hell knows redeeming,
But for souls sunk in seeming
    Fresh, till doomfire burn all,
120 Prayer shall fetch pity eternal.

Duns Scotus's Oxford

Towery city and branchy between towers;
Cuckoo-echoing, bell-swarmèd, lark-charmèd, rook-racked,
    river-rounded;
The dapple-eared lily below thee; that country and town did
Once encounter in, here coped and poisèd powers;

Thou hast a base and brickish skirt there, sours
That neighbour-nature thy grey beauty is grounded
Best in; graceless growth, thou has confounded
Rural rural keeping – folk, flocks, and flowers.

Yet ah! this air I gather and I release
He lived on; these weeds and waters, these walls are what
He haunted who of all men most sways my spirits to peace;

Of realty the rarest-veinèd unraveller; a not
Rivalled insight, be rival Italy or Greece;
Who fíred Fránce for Máry withóut spót.

Binsey Poplars
felled 1879

My aspens dear, whose airy cages quelled,
Quelled or quenched in leaves the leaping sun,
Áll félled, félled, are áll félled;
Of a fresh and following folded rank
Not spared, not one
That dandled a sandalled
Shadow that swam or sank
On meadow and river and wind-wandering weed-winding
bank.

O if we but knew what we do
10   When we delve or hew –
Hack and rack the growing green!
Since country is so tender
To tóuch, her béing só slénder,
That, like this sleek and seeing ball
But a prick will make no eye at all,
Where we, even where we mean
To mend her we end her,
When we hew or delve:
After-comers cannot guess the beauty been.
20   Ten or twelve, only ten or twelve
Strokes of havoc unselve
The sweet especial scene,
Rural scene, a rural scene,
Sweet especial rural scene.

Henry Purcell

The poet wishes well to the divine genius of Purcell and praises
him that, whereas other musicians have given utterance to the
moods of man's mind, he has, beyond that, uttered in notes the
very make and species of man as created both in him and in all
men generally

Have fáir fállen, O fáir, fáir have fállen, so déar
To me, so arch-especial a spirit as heaves in Henry Purcell,
An age is now since passed, since parted; with the reversal
Of the outward sentence low lays him, listed to a heresy,
    here.

Not mood in him nor meaning, proud fire or sacred fear,
Or love, or pity, or all that sweet notes not his might nursle:
It is the forgèd feature finds me; it is the rehearsal
Of own, of abrupt self there so thrusts on, so throngs the
    ear.

Let him oh! with his air of angels then lift me, lay me! only
    I'll
10   Have an eye to the sakes of him, quaint moonmarks, to his
    pelted plumage under
Wings: so some great stormfowl, whenever he has walked
    his while

The thunder-purple seabeach, plumèd purple-of-thunder,
If a wuthering of his palmy snow-pinions scatter a colossal
    smile
Off him, but meaning motion fans fresh our wits with
    wonder.

Peace

When will you ever, Peace, wild wooddove, shy wings shut,
Your round me roaming end, and under be my boughs?
When, when, Peace, will you, Peace? – I'll not play hypocrite

To own my heart: I yield you do come sometimes; but
That piecemeal peace is poor peace. What pure peace allows
Alarms of wars, the daunting, wars, the death of it?

O surely, reaving Peace, my Lord should leave in lieu
Some good! And so he does leave Patience exquisite,
That plumes to Peace thereafter. And when Peace here does
    house
10   He comes with work to do, he does not come to coo,
                He comes to brood and sit.

Felix Randal

Félix Rándal the fárrier, O is he déad then? my dúty all énded,
Who have watched his mould of man, big-boned and
    hardy-handsome
Pining, pining, till time when reason rambled in it and some
Fatal four disorders, fleshed there, all contended?

Sickness broke him. Impatient, he cursed at first, but mended
Being anointed and all; though a heavenlier heart began some
Mónths éarlier, since Í had our swéet repríeve and ránsom
Téndered to him. Áh well, God rést him áll road éver he
    offénded!

This séeing the síck endéars them tó us, us tóo it endéars.
My tongue had taught thee comfort, touch had quenched thy
    tears,
Thy tears that touched my heart, child, Felix, poor Felix
    Randal;

How far from then forethought of, all thy more boisterous
    years,
When thou at the random grim forge, powerful amidst peers,
Didst fettle for the great grey drayhorse his bright and battering
    sandal!

Spring and Fall:
to a Young Child

Margaret, are you grieving
Over Goldengrove unleaving?
Leaves, like the things of man, you
With your fresh thoughts care for, can you?
Ah! as the heart grows older
It will come to such sights colder
By and by, nor spare a sigh
Though worlds of wanwood leafmeal lie;
And yet you *will* weep and know why.
Now no matter, child, the name:
Sorrow's springs are the same.
Nor mouth had, no nor mind, expressed
What héart héard of, ghóst guéssed:
It is the blight man was born for,
It is Margaret you mourn for.

10

Inversnaid

This dárksome búrn, hórseback brówn,
His rollrock highroad roaring down,
In coop and in comb the fleece of his foam
Flutes and low to the lake falls home.

A wíndpuff-bónnet of fáwn-fróth
Turns and twindles over the broth
Of a póol so pitchblack, féll-frówning,
It rounds and rounds Despair to drowning.

10   Degged with dew, dappled with dew
Are the groins of the braes that the brook treads through,
Wiry heathpacks, flitches of fern,
And the beadbonny ash that sits over the burn.

What would the world be, once bereft
Of wet and of wildness? Let them be left,
O let them be left, wildness and wet;
Long live the weeds and the wilderness yet.

The Leaden Echo and the Golden Echo

(Maidens' song from *St Winefred's Well*)

The Leaden Echo –

How to keep – is there ány any, is there none such,
    nowhere known some, bow or brooch or braid or brace,
    lace, latch or catch or key to keep

Back beauty, keep it, beauty, beauty, beauty,… from
    vanishing away?

Ó is there no frowning of these wrinkles, rankèd wrinkles
    deep,

Down? no waving off of these most mournful messengers,
    still messengers, sad and stealing messengers of grey? –

No there's none, there's none, O no there's none,

Nor can you long be, what you now are, called fair,

Do what you may do, what, do what you may,

And wisdom is early to despair:

Be beginning; since, no, nothing can be done

To keep at bay

Age and age's evils, hoar hair,

Ruck and wrinkle, drooping, dying, death's worst, winding
    sheets, tombs and worms and tumbling to decay;

So be beginning, be beginning to despair.

O there's none; no no no there's none:

Be beginning to despair, to despair,

Despair, despair, despair, despair.

The Golden Echo –
Spare!

There is one, yes I have one (Hush there!);

Only not within seeing of the sun.

Not within the singeing of the strong sun,

Tall sun's tingeing, or treacherous the tainting of the
    earth's air,

Somewhere elsewhere there is ah well where! one,
One. Yes I can tell such a key, I do know such a place,
Where whatever's prizèd and passes of us, everything that's
    fresh and fast flying of us, seems to us sweet of us and
    swiftly away with, done away with, undone,
Undone, done with, soon done with, and yet dearly and
    dangerously sweet
Of us, the wimpledwater-dimpled, not-by morning-
    matchèd face,
The flower of beauty, fleece of beauty, too too apt to, ah! to
    fleet,
Never fleets more, fastened with the tenderest truth
To its own best being and its loveliness of youth: it is an
    everlastingness of, O it is an all youth!
Cóme then, your ways and airs and looks, locks,
    maidengear, gallantry and gaiety and grace,
Winning ways, airs innocent, maidenmanners, sweet
    looks, loose locks, long locks, lovelocks, gaygear, going
    gallant, girlgrace –
Resign them, sign them, seal them, send them, motion
    them with breath,
And with sighs soaring, soaring sighs, deliver
Them; beauty-in-the-ghost, deliver it, early now, long
    before death
Give beauty back, beauty, beauty, beauty, back to God
    beauty's self and beauty's giver.
See; not a hair is, not an eyelash, not the least lash lost;
    every hair
Is, hair of the head, numbéred.
Nay, what we had lighthanded left in surly the mere mould
Will have waked and have waxed and have walked with
    the wind what while we slept,
This side, that side hurling a heavy-headed hundredfold
What while we, while we slumbered.

O then, weary then whý should we tread? O why are we so
    haggard at the heart, so care-coiled, care-killed, so
    fagged, so fashed, so cogged, so cumbered,
When the thing we freely fórfeit is kept with fonder a care,
Fonder a care kept than we could have kept it, kept
Far with fonder a care (and we, we should have lost it)
    finer, fonder
30   A care kept. – Where kept? do but tell us where kept,
    where. –
    Yonder. – What high as that! We follow, now we follow. –
    Yonder, yes yonder, yonder,
Yonder.

Ribblesdale

Earth, sweet Earth, sweet landscape, with leavès throng
And louchèd low grass, heaven that dost appeal
To with no tongue to plead, no heart to feel;
That canst but only be, but dost that long –

Thou canst but be, but that thou well dost; strong
Thy plea with him who dealt, nay does now deal,
Thy lovely dale down thus and thus bids reel
Thy river, and o'er gives all to rack or wrong.

And what is Earth's eye, tongue, or heart else, where
10   Else, but in dear and dogged man? Ah, the heir
To his own selfbent so bound, so tied to his turn,

To thriftless reave both our rich round world bare
And none reck of world after, this bids wear
Earth brows of such care, care and dear concern.

The Blessed Virgin compared to the Air we Breathe

Wild air, world-mothering air,
Nestling me everywhere,
That each eyelash or hair
Girdles; goes home betwixt
The fleeciest, frailest-flixed
Snowflake; that's fairly mixed
With, riddles, and is rife
In every least thing's life;
This needful, never spent,
10   And nursing element;
My more than meat and drink,
My meal at every wink;
This air, which, by life's law,
My lung must draw and draw
Now but to breathe its praise,
Minds me in many ways
Of her who nót only
Gave God's infinity
Dwindled to infancy
20   Welcome in womb and breast,
Birth, milk, and all the rest
But mothers each new grace
That does now reach our race –
Mary Immaculate,
Merely a woman, yet
Whose presence, power is
Great as no goddess's
Was deemèd, dreamèd; who
This one work has to do –
30   Let all God's glory through,
God's glory which would go
Through her and from her flow

Off, and no way but so.
  I say that we are wound
With mercy round and round
As if with air: the same
Is Mary, more by name.
She, wild web, wondrous robe,
Mantles the guilty globe,
40 Since God has let dispense
Her prayers his providence:
Nay, more than almoner,
The sweet alms' self is her
And men are meant to share
Her life as life does air.
  If I have understood,
She holds high motherhood
Towards all our ghostly good
And plays in grace her part
50 About man's beating heart,
Laying, like air's fine flood,
The deathdance in his blood;
Yet no part but what will
Be Christ our Saviour still.
Of her flesh he took flesh:
He does take fresh and fresh,
Though much the mystery how,
Not flesh but spirit now
And makes, O marvellous!
60 New Nazareths in us,
Where she shall yet conceive
Him, morning, noon, and eve;
New Bethlems, and he born
There, evening, noon, and morn –
Bethlem or Nazareth,
Men here may draw like breath
More Christ and baffle death;
Who, born so, comes to be

New self and nobler me
70 In each one and each one
More makes, when all is done,
Both God's and Mary's Son.
    Again, look overhead
How air is azurèd;
O how! Nay do but stand
Where you can lift your hand
Skywards; rich, rich it laps
Round the four fingergaps.
Yet such a sapphire-shot,
80 Charged, steepèd sky will not
Stain light. Yea, mark you this:
It does no prejudice.
The glass-blue days are those
When every colour glows,
Each shape and shadow shows.
Blue be it: this blue heaven
The seven or seven times seven
Hued sunbeam will transmit
Perfect, not alter it.
90 Or if there does some soft,
On things aloof, aloft,
Bloom breathe, that one breath more
Earth is the fairer for.
Whereas did air not make
This bath of blue and slake
His fire, the sun would shake,
A blear and blinding ball
With blackness bound, and all
The thick stars round him roll
100 Flashing like flecks of coal,
Quartz-fret, or sparks of salt,
In grimy vasty vault.
    So God was god of old:
A mother came to mould

Those limbs like ours which are
What must make our daystar
Much dearer to mankind;
Whose glory bare would blind
Or less would win man's mind.
110 Through her we may see him
Made sweeter, not made dim,
And her hand leaves his light
Sifted to suit our sight.
Be thou then, O thou dear
Mother, my atmosphere;
My happier world, wherein
To wend and meet no sin;
Above me, round me lie
Fronting my froward eye
120 With sweet and scarless sky;
Stir in my ears, speak there
Of God's love, O live air,
Of patience, penance, prayer:
World-mothering air, air wild,
Wound with thee, in thee isled,
Fold home, fast fold thy child.

'To seem the stranger'

To seem the stranger lies my lot, my life
Among strangers. Father and mother dear,
Brothers and sisters are in Christ not near
And he my peace/my parting, sword and strife.

England, whose honour O all my heart woos, wife
To my creating thought, would neither hear
Me, were I pleading, plead nor do I: I wéar-
Y of idle a being but by where wars are rife.

I am in Ireland now; now I am at a thírd
10 Remove. Not but in all removes I can
Kind love both give and get. Only what word

Wisest my heart breeds dark heaven's baffling ban
Bars or hell's spell thwarts. This to hoard unheard,
Heard unheeded, leaves me a lonely began.

'I wake and feel'

I wake and feel the fell of dark, not day.
What hours, O what black hours we have spent
This night! what sights you, heart, saw; ways you went!
And more must, in yet longer light's delay.

With witness I speak this. But where I say
Hours I mean years, mean life. And my lament
Is cries countless, cries like dead letters sent
To dearest him that lives alas! away.

I am gall, I am heartburn. God's most deep decree
10 Bitter would have me taste: my taste was me;
Bones built in me, flesh filled, blood brimmed the curse.

Selfyeast of spirit a dull dough sours. I see
The lost are like this, and their scourge to be
As I am mine, their sweating selves; but worse.

55

'No worst'

No worst, there is none. Pitched past pitch of grief,
More pangs will, schooled at forepangs, wilder wring.
Comforter, where, where is your comforting?
Mary, mother of us, where is your relief?
My cries heave, herds-long; huddle in a main, a chief-
Woe, wórld-sorrow; on an áge-old ánvil wínce and síng –
Then lull, then leave off. Fury had shrieked 'No ling-
Ering! Let me be fell: force I must be brief.'
O the mind, mind has mountains; cliffs of fall
Frightful, sheer, no-man-fathomed. Hold them cheap
May who ne'er hung there. Nor does long our small
Durance deal with that steep or deep. Here! creep,
Wretch, under a comfort serves in a whirlwind: all
Life death does end and each day dies with sleep.

To what serves Mortal Beauty?

To what serves mortal beauty – | dangerous; does set danc-
Ing blood – the O-seal-that-so | feature, flung prouder form
Than Purcell tune lets tread to? | See: it does this: keeps
    warm
Men's wit to the things that are; | to what good means –
    where a glance
Master more may than gaze, | gaze out of countenance.
Those lovely lads once, wet-fresh | windfalls of war's storm,
How then should Gregory, a father, | have gleanèd else
    from swarm-
Èd Rome? But God to a nation | dealt that day's dear
    chance.
To man, that once would worship | block or barren stone,
Our law says / love what are | love's worthiest, were all
    known;

World's loveliest – men's selves. Self | flashes off frame and
    face.
What do then? how meet beauty? | Merely meet it; own,
Home at heart, heaven's sweet gift; | then leave, let that
    alone.
Yea, wish that though, wish all, | God's better beauty, grace.

(The Soldier)

YES. Whý do we áll, séeing of a | soldier, bless him? bléss
Our redcoats, our tars? Both | thése being, the greater part,
But frail clay, nay but foul clay. | Hére it is: the heart,
Since, proud, it calls the calling | manly, gives a guess
That, hopes that, mákesbelieve, | the men must be no less;
It fancies, feigns, deems, déars | the artist after his art;
And fain will find as sterling | all as all is smart
And scarlet wéar the spirit of war thére express.
Mark Christ our King. He knows war, served this
    soldiering through;
10 He of all can handle a rope best. | There he bides in bliss
Now, and séeing somewhére some mán| do all that man can do,
For love he léans forth, needs | his neck must fall on, kiss,
And cry 'O Christ-done deed! | So God-made-flesh does too:
Were I come o'er again' cries | Christ 'it should be this'.

(Carrion Comfort)

Not, I'll not, carrion comfort, Despair, not feast on thee;
Not untwist – slack they may be – these last strands of man
In me ór, most weary, cry *I can no more*. I can;
Can something, hope, wish day come, not choose not to be.

But ah, but O thou terrible, why wouldst thou rude on me
Thy wring-earth right foot rock? lay a lionlimb against me?
    scan
With darksome devouring eyes my bruisèd bones? and fan,
O in turns of tempest, me heaped there; me frantic to avoid
    thee and flee?

Why? That my chaff might fly; my grain lie, sheer and clear.
Nay in all that toil, that coil, since (seems) I kissed the rod,
Hand rather, my heart lo! lapped strength, stole joy, would
    laugh, cheer.

Cheer whóm though? The héro whose héaven-handling
    flúng me, fóot tród
Me? or mé that fóught him? O whích one? is it eách one?
    That níght, that year
Of now done darkness I wretch lay wrestling with (my
    God!) my God.

'Patience, hard thing'

Patience, hard thing! the hard thing but to pray,
But bid for, patience is! Patience who asks
Wants war, wants wounds; weary his times, his tasks;
To do without, take tosses, and obey.

Rare patience roots in these, and, these away,
No-where. Natural heart's-ivy Patience masks
Our ruins of wrecked past purpose. There she basks
Purple eyes and seas of liquid leaves all day.

We hear our hearts grate on themselves: it kills
10   To bruise them dearer. Yet the rebellious wills
Of us wé do bid God bend to him even so.

And where is he who more and more distills
Delicious kindness? – He is patient. Patience fills
His crisp combs, and that comes those ways we know.

'My own heart'

My own heart let me more have pity on; let
Me live to my sad self hereafter kind,
Charitable; not live this tormented mind
With this tormented mind tormenting yet.

I cast for comfort I can no more get
By groping round my comfortless than blind
Eyes in their dark can day or thirst can find
Thirst's all-in-all in all a world of wet.

Soul, self; come, poor Jackself, I do advise
10   You, jaded, lét be; call off thoughts awhile
Elsewhere; leave comfort root-room; let joy size

At God knows when to God knows what; whose smile
'S not wrung, see you; unforseentimes rather – as skies
Betweenpie mountains – lights a lovely mile.

Spelt from Sibyl's Leaves

Earnest, earthless, equal, attuneable, | vaulty,
    voluminous,… stupendous
Evening strains to be tíme's vást, | womb-of-all, home-
    of-all, hearse-of-all night.
Her fond yellow hornlight wound to the west, | her wild
    hollow hoarlight hung to the height
Waste; her earliest stars, earlstars, | stars principal,
    overbend us,
Fíre-féaturing héaven. For éarth | her béing has
    unboúnd; her dápple is at énd, as-
Tray or aswarm, all throughther, in throngs; | self ín self
    stéepèd and páshed – qúite
Disremembering, dismembering | all now. Heart, you
    round me right
With: Óur évening is óver us; óur night | whélms,
    whélms, ánd will énd us.
Only the beakleaved boughs dragonish | damask the
    tool-smooth bleak light; black,
10   Ever so black on it. Óur tale, O óur oracle! | Lét life,
    wáned, ah lét life wínd
Off hér once skéined stained véined varíety | upon, áll
    on twó spools; párt, pen, páck
Now her áll in twó flocks, twó folds – bláck, white; |
    ríght, wrong; réckon but, réck but, mínd
But thése two; wáre of a wórld where bút these | twó tell,
    eách off the óther; of a ráck
Where, selfwrung, selfstrung, sheathe- and shelterless, |
    thoúghts agáinst thoughts ín groans grínd.

Harry Ploughman

Hard as hurdle arms, with a broth of goldish flue
Breathed round; the rack of ribs; the scooped flank; lank
Rope-over thigh; knee-nave; and barrelled shank –
　　　　Head and foot, shouldér and shank –
By a grey eye's heed steered well, one crew, fall to;
Stand at stress. Each limb's barrowy brawn, his thew
That onewhere curded, onewhere sucked or sank –
　　　　Soared ór sank –
Though as a beechbole firm, finds his, as at a rollcall, rank
And features, in flesh, what deed he each must do –
　　　　His sinew-service where do.
He leans to it, Harry bends, look. Back, elbow, and liquid
　　waist
In him, all quáil to the wallowing o'the plough. 'S cheek
　　crímsons; curls
Wag or crossbridle, in a wind lifted, windlaced –
　　　　　　Wind-lilylocks-laced;
Churlsgrace too, chíld of Amansstrength, how it hángs or
　　hurls
Them – broad in bluff hide his frowning feet lashed!
　　raced
With, along them, cragiron under and cold furls –
　　　　With-a-fountain's shining-shot furls.

Tom's Garland:
upon the Unemployed

Tom – garlanded with squat and surly steel
Tom; then Tom's fallowbootfellow piles pick
By him and rips out rockfire homeforth – sturdy Dick;
Tom Heart-at-ease, Tom Navvy: he is all for his meal
Sure, 's bed now. Low be it: lustily he his low lot (feel
That ne'er need hunger, Tom; Tom seldom sick,
Seldomer heartsóre; that treads through, prickproof, thick
Thousands of thorns, thoughts) swings though.
    Commonweal
Little Í reck ho! lacklevel in, if all had bread:
What! Country is honour enough in all us – lordly head,
With heaven's lights high hung round, or, mother-ground
That mammocks, mighty foot. But nö way sped,
Nor mind nor mainstrength; gold go garlanded
With, perilous, O nó; nor yet plod safe shod sound;
                  Undenizened, beyond bound
Of earth's glory, earth's ease, all; no-one, nowhere,
In wide the world's weal; rare gold, bold steel, bare
             In both; care, but share care –
This, by Despair, bred Hangdog dull; by Rage,
Manwolf, worse; and their packs infest the age.

That Nature is a Heraclitean Fire and of the comfort of the Resurrection

Cloud-puffball, torn tufts, tossed pillows | flaunt forth, then
    chevy on an air –
Built thoroughfare: heaven-roysterers, in gay-gangs | they
    throng; they glitter in marches.
Down roughcast, down dazzling whitewash, | wherever an
    elm arches,
Shivelights and shadowtackle in long | lashes lace, lance,
    and pair.
Delightfully the bright wind boisterous | ropes, wrestles,
    beats earth bare
Of yestertempest's creases; in pool and rutpeel parches
Squandering ooze to squeezed | dough, crust, dust; stanches,
    starches
Squadroned masks and manmarks | treadmire toil there
Footfretted in it. Million-fuelèd, | nature's bonfire burns on.
10 But quench her bonniest, dearest | to her, her clearest-
    selvèd spark
Man, how fast his firedint, | his mark on mind, is gone!
Both are in an únfathomable, all is in an enormous dark
Drowned. O pity and indig | nation! Manshape, that shone
Sheer off, disseveral, a star | death blots black out; nor mark
    Is any of him at all so stark
But vastness blurs and time | beats level. Enough! the
    Resurrection,
A heart's-clarion! Away grief's gasping, | joyless days,
    dejection.
                    Across my foundering deck shone
A beacon, an eternal beam. | Flesh fade, and mortal trash
20 Fall to the residuary worm; | world's wildfire, leave but ash:
              In a flash, at a trumpet crash,

I am all at once what Christ is, | since he was what I am, and
This Jack, joke, poor potsherd, | patch, matchwood, immortal diamond,
                Is immortal diamond.

Justus quidem tu es, Domine,

si disputem tecum; verumtamen justa loquar ad te:
quare via impiorum prosperatur? etc (Jerem. xii 1)

Thou art indeed just, Lord, if I contend
With thee; but, sir, so what I plead is just.
Why do sinners' ways prosper? and why must
Disappointment all I endeavour end?

Wert thou my enemy, O thou my friend,
How wouldst thou worse, I wonder, than thou dost
Defeat, thwart me? Oh, the sots and thralls of lust
Do in spare hours more thrive than I that spend,

Sir, life upon thy cause. See, banks and brakes
10 Now, leavèd how thick! lacèd they are again
With fretty chervil, look, and fresh wind shakes

Them; birds build – but not I build; no, but strain,
Time's eunuch, and not breed one work that wakes.
Mine, O thou lord of life, send my roots rain.

'The shepherd's brow'

The shepherd's brow, fronting forked lightning, owns
The horror and the havoc and the glory
Of it. Angels fall, they are towers, from heaven – a story
Of just, majestical, and giant groans.
But man – we, scaffold of score brittle bones;
Who breathe, from groundlong babyhood to hoary
Age gasp; whose breath is our *memento mori* –
What bass is *our* viol for tragic tones?
He! Hand to mouth he lives, and voids with shame;
And, blazoned in however bold the name,
Man Jack the man is, just; his mate a hussy.
And I that die these deaths, that feed this flame,
That... in smooth spoons spy life's masque mirrored: tame
My tempests there, my fire and fever fussy.

To R. B.

The fine delight that fathers thought; the strong
Spur, live and lancing like the blowpipe flame,
Breathes once and, quenchèd faster than it came,
Leaves yet the mind a mother of immortal song.

Nine months she then, nay years, nine years she long
Within her wears, bears, cares and combs the same:
The widow of an insight lost she lives, with aim
Now known and hand at work now never wrong.

Sweet fire the sire of muse, my soul needs this;
I want the one rapture of an inspiration.
O then if in my lagging lines you miss

The roll, the rise, the carol, the creation,
My winter world, that scarcely breathes that bliss
Now, yields you, with some sighs, our explanation.

65

Notes

Heaven-Haven

Note the subtitle (*a nun takes the veil*): to 'take the veil' is to make the vows or formal commitment a woman makes when becoming a nun. The poem is of interest on several counts: its form and idiom are very different from the style of most of the poems in this selection, and yet certain elements are highly characteristic of Hopkins. The title is an example of the kind of sound-play which distinguishes his 'voice' as a writer. The nun speaking in the text is a *persona*; an 'I' who is not the author in his or her real life, a created character speaking in the first person. Perhaps this is the nearest to spiritual self-disclosure the twenty-year-old Hopkins, still an undergraduate at Balliol College Oxford, chose to come.

> 5–8 The contrasted imagery: *sea* (8) for spiritual unrest and *havens* (7) for peace, anticipates the ambitious use of the sea as a spiritual symbol that we find in his two longest poems, *The Wreck of the Deutschland* and *The Loss of the Eurydice*.

The Habit of Perfection

Look at the title; how many different senses of the word 'habit' can you think of? How many of those senses might be relevant here?

This is another early text, with a religious context established. It shows Hopkins's interest in paradox – ideas that seem to contradict each other being sustained at the same time. Here, the idea that *Elected Silence* (1) should be *The music that I care to hear* (4). Again, there are interesting anticipations of the concerns in his later writing; above all, the stress on the senses and the (rather pious?) belief that they are best directed to aspects of the material world linked to the divine – the taste of bread when fasting, the odour of incense on an altar.

That said, the poem displays a verbal energy that looks forward more directly than *Heaven-Haven* to the style of later poems. Phrases such as *This ruck and reel* (11) and *Palate, the hutch of tasty lust,* (13) are using sound combinations to force associations on us as readers, a key element in the stylistic repertoire of the later Hopkins. (On this, see Interpretations pp. 144–45.)

1 **Elected Silence** For the mystics, cultivating silence and withdrawal from the world was a pre-condition for communication with God. In a letter written about the same time as this poem (September 1866), Hopkins wrote that *silence is an excellent discipline and especially during the process of conviction.*

6 **curfew** Is this meant to suggest martial law, a silence strictly imposed?

10 **uncreated light** another idea from the mystics – a spiritual light, visible only to the soul, not the physical eye.

19 **censers** vessels for burning incense in a religious ritual or ceremony.

20 **sanctuary side** part of a church containing the high altar.

21 **O feel-of-primrose hands** One feature of the mature Hopkins style is a taste for vivid-sounding, made-up compound adjectives, as here.

22 **plushy sward** a reminder of where Hopkins came from as a writer; a dead and clichéd phrase, even in the mid-1860s?

24 **unhouse and house the Lord** The tabernacle on the altar of a Catholic church 'houses' the consecrated host, the wafer of bread which believers regard as becoming the body of Christ during the sacrament of the Mass.

25 **And, Poverty... bride** St Francis of Assisi, the medieval mystic, regarded himself as married to 'poverty'.

The Wreck of the Deutschland

As with *The Windhover*, the Notes on this poem have been kept largely to specific words or phrases. There is a discussion in the Interpretations (pp. 157–62) of the poem's central relevance to Hopkins's work.

Notes

Part the first

1 **mastering**   key word. Remember that the *Deutschland*'s
captain was also her 'master'.

3 **strand**   beach.

sway   two possible senses here: motion (surge of the sea) or
control (holding sway). The 'marine' references hint at the
coming narrative focus in Part the second.

5 **Thou hast... flesh**   very close to Job 10:11, an Old Testament
text obsessed with the issue of human suffering and the place it
occupies in a world created by a loving and strong God: *Thou
hast clothed me with skin and flesh, and hast fenced me with bones
and sinews.*

8 **I feel thy finger... find**   The alliterated *f* draws attention to the
disturbing sense of God's power, of inescapable divine probing
and enquiry.

10 **lightning and lashed rod**   here, symbols of divine power and
(punishing) authority; *say yes* (9) underlines Hopkins's
acceptance. (See the sonnets *God's Grandeur*, p. 31 and *(Carrion
Comfort)*, p. 58 for other uses of *rod* in connection with
submission to divine authority.)

15 **horror of height**   Hopkins may or may not have suffered the
agonies of vertigo, but it is interesting that later in his life, in a
similar context evoking spiritual stress and disorientation, he
also expresses his mental distress through a 'vertiginous' image.
(See the sonnet *'No worst'*, p. 56 and the Notes on p. 104.)

19 **a place**   of escape from the terrors described above.

20 **spell**   during that time.

21 **the heart of the Host**   i.e. to Christ as represented in the
Host, the consecrated bread used in the communion service.

22–3 **dovewinged... Carrier-witted**   Hopkins addresses his own
heart, his deepest emotional and spiritual instincts, regarding
them as both peace-loving *(dovewinged)* and with a sure instinct
for God, like homing pigeons *(Carrier-witted)*.

24 God is present both in the terror from which Hopkins escapes
and in the peace he eventually embraces – a basic theme of the
poem.

26–7 Hopkins describes his own condition as outwardly stable but,
like fine sand inexorably falling through an hour-glass, basically
escaping, disintegrating; *mined* (27) may be taken as Hopkins's
shorthand for 'undermined'.

68

28 **combs to the fall** Waves can be said to *comb*, reach their high point then fall over; here is a metaphor linking water (everpresent in Part the first) to the sand racing through the hour-glass.

29 **poise... pane** equilibrium; a flat, calm surface.

30 **roped with** secured by, picking up the vertigo images of lines 14–15.

31 **voel** Welsh term for hill (in Welsh, 'foel', pronounced 'voil'), used here for sound (alliterating with *vein*) as well as rhythm.

32 **gospel proffer** the gospel offer or promise, i.e. the chance of redemption from sin, eternal life in Heaven, which Hopkins regards himself in line 30 as *roped with*.

33 **kiss my hand** image of (chivalrous) courtesy and affection.

34 **lovely-asunder** invented compound term; both lovely and separate, distinct from each other (*lovely* because separate?).

35 **him** i.e. Christ.

37 **dappled** compare with *Pied Beauty*, (p. 35, 1).
   damson a dark purple shade.

38 The key term here is *under*. Christ is part of the divine sustaining force in all of nature, but a presence implicit rather than explicit: this helps to clarify lines 39–40.

39 **His mystery** Christ simultaneously man and God is the *mystery*, a religious truth not capable of rational explanation or analysis.
   instressed suggests the true **inscape** of starlight and sunsets is inseparable from God.

48 **fable** invent fictions, stories (i.e. to account for the world without acknowledging a creating God).

50 **his going in Galilee** from the time, after his resurrection from the grave, that Christ finally ascended back to Heaven.

51 **Warm-laid... grey** paradox again suggesting *mystery* (see Note on line 39); more conventionally we might link *grave* (death) with *grey*, *womb-life* with *Warm*.

52 **Manger, maiden's knee** images of Christ's birth and rearing, the *Manger* being the inn stable at Bethlehem where he was born, the *maiden's knee* belonging to Mary his mother.

53 **Passion** the sufferings of Christ prior to his death as recorded in the gospels.

59 **sloe** comparing the believer's spiritual experience of Christ to the powerful sensory experience of eating a ripe sloe, a wild

plum with a distinctive bitter-sweet taste. The verbal technique in lines 58–62 strongly suggests the influence of 'Cynghanedd' (see Interpretations p. 144).

63 **hero of Calvary** Christ, crucified on the hill of Calvary.

66 **three-numbered form** in Christian theology, God is seen as three persons in one identity: God the Father, God the Son and God the Holy Spirit.

67–8 Again, as in the opening lines, Hopkins manages to suggest the context of the narrative of Part the second through the phrase *wrecking and storm*.

70 **lightning... warm** God as extremes; apparent contradictions; opposites (like the bitter-sweet sloe). Hence the idea of paradox: two apparently contradictory notions or ideas affirmed at the same time, extended here into lines 71–2.

73–4 **anvil-ding... will** one type of divine interaction with individuals expressed in images of dramatic force and heat (like a blacksmith), strongly contrasted with a gentler, more insinuating effect in lines 75–6.

77 **Paul** St Paul, converted from a life persecuting believers by an abrupt appearance by God on the road to Damascus, recounted in Acts of the Apostles 9.

78 **Austin** St Augustine, converted to Christianity in a far less explosive way, as described in his own *Confessions*.

80 **Mastery... King** Note how the stressed words at the end of Part the first relate directly to power and authority, linking back to the opening phrase of Part the first (*Thou mastering me/God!* 1–2) and re-emphasizing Hopkins's sense of the need to worship (*but be adored*) this all-powerful deity.

Part the second

82 **The flange and the rail** (topical) reference to deaths caused through railway accidents at the time the poem was written (the 1870s); the flange is the projecting rim of the wheel which fits on the railway track.

83–4 Death personified here in military terms (*drum* and *bugle*) as the recruiting sergeant.

88 **sour** nasty.
cringe The scythe, traditional tool of Death the Grim Reaper, makes the meadow flowers buckle, give way.

blear share   the unseeing ploughshare; the assonantal chime (*ear/are*) is very much a feature of Hopkins's idiom.

93 **O Father**   God.

not under thy feathers   not protected or sheltered.

94 **the doom**   the fate; there is a link with *goal* at the start of the line; both words imply a pre-ordained final target. (Compare with Note to line 224.)

95 **the bay of thy blessing**   *bay* is an architectural term for recess.

96 **vault**   cover.

rounds   is the difficult word in this context, but perhaps the basic sense is *rounds* as in series, cycles or as in allowance, distribution.

reeve   fasten, attach.

98 **Hurling**   Does this imply that Hopkins sees the ship as deliberately giving up the chance of safety?

the haven   shelter, either in a harbour or from a lee shore.

104 **widow-making... deeps**   Notice the sequence of verbal adjectives here, each implying the sea as an environment actively hostile to humans.

107 **combs**   ridges on the sandbank.

108 **Dead**   meaning both 'exactly' and 'fatally'.

Kentish Knock   sandbank near the mouth of the Thames estuary.

109 **bows... keel**   the front of the ship; the timbers/steel plates of its underside.

110 **beam**   broadest cross-section of the ship.

111 **whorl**   propeller.

115 **Trenched with tears**   Following on from the personification of an abstract term, *Hope*, in the previous two lines, does this line involve exaggerated or inflated images?

117 A line which draws attention through the blend of alliteration in the *f* and *l* sounds alongside strong internal rhymes: *fright*, *night* and *ful, fall, ful*.

120 **the shrouds**   the rigging of the ship's sails, but also as in burial shroud.

125 **dreadnought breast**   an image for a strong sailor; a dreadnought was a heavy battleship.

braids of thew   *braids* are plaited lengths of hair; *thew* is muscle or sinew, so an image of a well-muscled character.

Compare this with the appreciation of muscular build reflected in the late sonnet *Harry Ploughman* (p. 61).

127 **cobbled foam-fleece** alliterative with the *f* and *l* sounds, and also a strongly visual metaphor; the white foam from the crashing seas resembles both wool and the massed, hard shape of street cobbles, far more familiar to Hopkins than to us.

128 **burl** literally, a lump in a piece of cloth.

129 **God's cold** Why might describing the *cold* as *God's* be significant in the overall argument of the poem?

133 **Night roared** extra impact from imagining night itself as howling, rather than those trapped on the ship?

135 **a lioness** The tall nun whose prayer calling on Christ was mentioned in the contemporary news reports, seizes Hopkins's imagination.

136 **virginal tongue** *virginal* due to taking a lifelong vow of chastity.

137 **bower of bone** A *bower* is literally a dwelling place, a home – here the human body; it is characteristic of Hopkins to use vividly alliterative terms like this to present a visual, tactile image. (Compare with *bone-house* in *The Caged Skylark*, p. 35, 2.)

138 **you** the nun? us, as his readers? Who do you think is being addressed through the dramatic exclamations at the start of this and the following two lines? Does it make sense to see this *you* as being the same as the *heart* spoken to in line 140?

141 The apparent contradiction Hopkins underlines here is fundamental to the Christian idea of human nature as a paradox: made in the image of God, so capable of perfection, but also corrupt and liable to sin, via free will.

142 **a madrigal start!** *start* is any sudden show of feeling or emotion; *madrigal*, an elaborately composed song for several voices without instrumental accompaniment, often associated with the Elizabethan period. It may be easiest to interpret this as a synonym for the preceding word, *melting*, insinuatingly beautiful sound.

146 **master** i.e. Christ; but the echo of 'master' as ship's captain too.

147 **hawling** combining howling and brawling?

148 **The rash smart sloggering brine** *brine* is the salt water of the *inboard* seas of the previous line; *rash* has direct associations with boldness, impetuosity, while *smart* conveys the stinging

effect on the face of the salt water carried on strong winds. *Sloggering* is probably a Hopkins invention; it is up to you to decide what kind of verbal, sound associations the word contains ('slog' as in hit, thump?).

150 **one fetch** a single, all-absorbing goal.

151 **tall nun** It seems likely that Hopkins knew that this was also a technical term for a distinctively shaped maritime buoy. Does the pun (if you see one here) indicate macabre humour?

154 **coifed** wearing coifs, the cap covering a nun's head.

155 **double a desperate name!** because Germany (Deutschland) expelled the nuns and the ship has left them all exposed to the threat of a terrible death.

157 **Gertrude, lily and Luther** St Gertrude was a Benedictine nun, a saintly mystic, pure and holy (*lily* is a Christian symbol of purity); Luther was a principal figure of the European Reformation, and for Hopkins a symbol of evil – *beast of the waste wood* in the next line. The irony is that both were closely associated with the German town of Eisleben (hence *two of a town*). As in line 141, Hopkins reflects on the co-existence of good and evil in the world.

160 For the story of Cain and Abel, see Genesis 4.

163 **Rhine... Thames** *Rhine* as a symbol for Germany, while *Thames* is used in a literal sense; the ship has been wrecked on a sandbank in the Thames estuary.

165 **Gnashed** suggesting the almost conscious violence of the elements, the metaphor implied being that of hunting dogs. (See the rest of the line and the Note on Orion.)
Orion of light In astronomy, Orion is a constellation named after the hunter in Greek mythology slain by the goddess Diana. As Orion was associated with stormy weather the relevance here is clear enough. If God is the hunter, and the savage elements combining to wreck the ship and drown its passengers and crew are the hunter's dogs, again we see Hopkins taking on the issue of human suffering being allowed, somehow even caused, by a loving God.

166 **unchancelling** another example of Hopkins inventing a strong adjective; the chancel is that part of a church housing the altar and choir, so in one sense *unchancelling* means: taking (the nuns) from their religious environment (through expulsion

from their German convent). But another meaning of 'chancel' is the door-screen through which nuns in enclosed orders can greet any visitors from the outside world. The nuns have been 'unchancelled' in the sense that they gain greater fame from their deaths than they would ever have expected or desired. The two senses are complementary rather than exclusive.

167 **Thou martyr-master**   i.e. God.

168 The hostile, deadly elements of the storm altered into symbols of pure beauty by God's vision in eternity.

169 **Five!**   Numbers are symbolically important in many religious contexts: three the trinity, seven the deadly sins, ten the commandments, twelve the Apostles and so on. *Five* is significant because it represents the wounds on the body of Christ after the Crucifixion. And of course five is the number of the nuns trapped on board the *Deutschland*.
finding   emblem, special sign.
sake   that aspect of a thing which most distinguishes it besides physical shape or appearance. (See the sonnet *Henry Purcell*, p. 43, 10 and the Note on p. 95.)

170 **cipher**   secret symbol.

171 **Mark... mark**   The first is an imperative 'Take note!', the second the noun.

173 **scores it in scarlet**   inflicts bleeding wounds.
bespoken   i.e. Christ's own sufferings are inflicted on those closest to him, most loved by him.

174 **Before-time-taken**   predestined, chosen before they existed to suffer as part of the overall divine plan.

175 **Stigma, signal, cinquefoil token**   The stigma is a mark that sets its bearer aside (compare with 'stigmatized'); specifically, the stigmata are the marks of the nails, lance etc. which Catholics believe certain especially holy individuals bear: e.g. St Francis of Assisi, as mentioned in lines 177–81. *Cinquefoil* describes any five-leaved decoration, while *token*, like *signal*, is something that points to or stands for something else – here, the idea of Christ's suffering on behalf of mankind.

176 **the lamb's fleece**   Christ as the sacrificial lamb, symbol of innocence.
ruddying of the rose-flake   As the lily is a Christian symbol of purity, so the rose is a symbol of martyrdom.

177 **father Francis**   The nuns were Franciscans, members of the religious order established by St Francis of Assisi. (See link with stigmata in Note to line 175.)

180 **Lovescape crucified**   *lovescape* is probably an outward sign or show of the love in the Hopkins idiom, directly linked to **inscape**.

181 **seal of his seraph-arrival!**   The fact that St Francis received the signs of the Crucifixion was proof (*seal*) of his entry into Heaven. A seraph is one of the higher orders of angels.

184 Again the co-existence of opposites: *fall-gold mercies* juxtaposed with *all-fire glances*; God the merciful father, God the all-powerful judge.

185–7 **Away... rest**   Hopkins turning abruptly to his own situation, tranquil and comfortable in St Beuno's College at the very time the nuns were in such distress at sea on the other side of the country. What is the effect on the narrative of this sudden change of scene? Does Hopkins mention his own situation as a way of heightening the anguish of the nuns, or as a way of implying his sense of guilt that they should suffer while he was tucked up in bed? Which seems likelier?

192 **christens her wild-worst Best**   Holding a crucifix to her breast, the nun makes what is apparently the worst experience of her life the best by offering up her imminent death to God as a sacrifice. To christen – whether a baby or an experience (as here) – is to admit something into the realm of God.

194 **arch and original Breath**   the spirit of God that first breathed life into the Creation. (See Genesis 1.)

196 **body of lovely Death**   i.e. Christ crucified; *lovely* because through Christ's suffering and death, mankind regained the hope of eternal life in Heaven which was lost through Adam's original sin.

197–8 **the men... Gennésaréth**   nothing directly to do with the *Deutschland*; this is a reference to the story of Christ, his disciples and the turbulent waters of the Sea of Galilee (Matthew 8). Terrified of drowning, the disciples call upon the sleeping Christ to save them; Christ calms the waters, but not before rebuking the men for their lack of faith. The relevance to this context? Is Hopkins suggesting a comparison between the nun and the timid disciples?

199 **the crown** Traditionally, the martyr's reward of eternal life in Heaven for enduring pain and death on earth for Christ's sake was symbolized as a crown.

200 The greater her distress and suffering, the more eager she becomes to gain eternal life.

203 **jay-blue** One element in a jay's plumage is a rich blue; there are several examples in his poems of the intense pleasure Hopkins derived from experiencing the various blues of the sky. In a letter to R. W. Dixon he remarked that *crimson and pure blues seemed to me spiritual and heavenly sights fit to draw tears once*. For references to blue skies in the poems, look for instance at *The Blessed Virgin compared to the Air we Breathe* (p. 51) and the sonnet *Spring* (p. 32).

204 **pied** multi-coloured. (Compare with *Pied Beauty*, p. 35.)

206 **belled fire** Is this a reference to the light of the stars, and if so, why *belled*?

moth-soft a surprisingly tactile image following on from something more visual.

208 **The... hearing** an echo of St Paul's First Epistle to the Corinthians 2; the reference is to Heaven.

209–16 This stanza is discussed in the Interpretations pp. 158–60.

217 Here the tone changes as suddenly as the rhythm itself. Why?

221 **Ipse** Latin term for He, himself (Christ); Latin because of its associations with the language of the Mass, with the Latin Bible (the Vulgate)? Or because Hopkins needs two stresses rather than one (pronounced *ip-say*)?

224 **doom** judgement or decision; often associated in Christian thinking with the Last Judgement at the end of time, the Apocalypse, when all mankind will be rewarded or punished according to their merits. (See Note to line 94.)

226 **single eye** *single* in the sense exclusively focused on; an image of the nun's intense concentration.

227 **unshapeable shock night** compacted sense once more; the shocks experienced in the night are so traumatic they cannot be explained, made sense of, accounted for (i.e. 'shaped' in the sense of rationally ordered).

231 **The Simon Peter of a soul!** Peter here has the image of the true believer, the *rock* on which Christ said he would build his church (Matthew 16:18).

232 **Tarpeïan-fast**   The Tarpeïan rock was a cliff outside Rome; *fast* here in the sense immovable, holding firm. St Peter was the first Pope; the Pope as spiritual head of the Catholic faith on earth lived in Rome. This is the kind of idea sequence Hopkins is suggesting here.
beacon of light   at once symbolic – the Church as the (spiritual) light of the world – and concrete, *beacon* as in lighthouse beacon, apposite for a ship drifted onto treacherous sandbanks.

234 **maid's son**   *maid* as in virgin; Christ as Mary's son, conceived uniquely without losing her virginity – hence Immaculate Conception and the reference in line 237 to *the one woman without stain.*

235 **feast**   The ship was wrecked on the night of 7 December; the next day is the feast-day in the Catholic Church of the Immaculate Conception, so Hopkins is drawing spiritual links between the glorious end of the brave nun and the celebration of the Virgin Mary, herself a symbol for all nuns. (See the Notes to *The Blessed Virgin compared to the Air we Breathe* (p. 101.)

241 **she has thee for the pain**   The nun has an eternal reward in Heaven for the sufferings she and her fellows have endured on board ship. Hopkins goes on to contrast her fate with that of those on board, *Comfortless unconfessed* (244).

245 **lovely-felicitous Providence**   See Interpretations pp. 161–63 for comment on this phrase and its significance within the overall framework of the poem.

246 **Finger**   See line 8: *Over again I feel thy finger and find thee.*

248 **poor sheep**   those sailors and fellow-passengers on board the ship who may have received the grace to save them from eternal punishment through the prayers of the nun.

249 **thee**   God, as discovered through nature. In this prayerful context, it may be helpful to note that *admire* can mean 'wonder at', 'be amazed by', as well as 'respect', 'look up to'.

250 **the Yore-flood**   three possible senses, all appropriate in this context: the ocean; the waters of Creation (Genesis 1); the flood from which Noah was saved (Genesis 7).

251 **The recurb**   another Hopkins coinage; God's renewed control of the tides?

252 the extent of the oceans and their confining edges against land.

253 a movement to the metaphorical *ocean* of the individual's mind.

254 **Ground... granite** stressing the believer's sense of God as the source and support of his existence, the alliterated *gr* sound used to be forceful, aggressive?

254–5 **past all/Grasp God** God who cannot, physically and intellectually, be restricted by human powers; the kind of compound adjective Hopkins invents so frequently in his verse.

256 **heeds but hides, bodes but abides** God the unseen observer, knowing everything still to occur in the course of history but letting it take its preordained path; a basic aspect both of Hopkins's own religious outlook and of the ideas sustaining this text, characteristically channelled here through alliterated half-rhymes.

257 **outrides** transcends, goes beyond.

258 **ark** here a symbol of security from (spiritual) destruction.

259 **the lingerer with a love** Christ, whose love and mercy reaches as far as the souls trapped in Purgatory.

261 **pent** locked up, trapped.

266 **Double-natured name** Christ, by nature both God and man.

267 **maiden-furled** enclosed in the Virgin's womb; all the descriptive phrases here and in line 268 are applied to Christ, described cumulatively in line 269 as *Mid-numbered he*, the mid-term of the Holy Trinity: Father, Son and Holy Spirit.

270 **dooms-day** See Note to line 224.

272 God's intervention in the natural world through this shipwreck has not been the kind of huge disruption of all order that will accompany the Last Judgement; *flash to the shire* implies a more local revelation.

273 **Dame** Hopkins ends the poem with a stanza in the form of a prayer to the dead nun, addressed here as *Dame*.
At our door near us (Britons), as in just offshore, but also hinting at moral responsibility (why were the exiled nuns not seeking a haven in Britain?).

275 **heaven-haven** Hopkins used the same phrase earlier in his career as the title of a short lyric about a nun taking the veil (see p. 16 and related Note p. 66); looking again at that lyric, do you think that the verbal link is deliberate or coincidental?

277 **easter in us**   good example of Hopkins's talent for coining
       powerful words, here a noun transformed to a verb. From the
       context, what might 'eastering' involve?
       crimson-cresseted   A cresset is a vessel used with oil or coal
       as a light, often as a signal; *crimson* may simply be a colour
       reference to a beautiful sunrise, itself a symbol of new life, new
       beginnings, but it may also have blood/sacrificial overtones; do
       you consider this would be a far-fetched reading of the phrase?

278–9 Christ as the freshly rising sun; light defeating darkness is
       among the most basic of all images where natural phenomena
       are used to convey symbolic meanings (physical daylight
       standing for good, night/darkness for evil and ignorance).

280 The poem ends with an extraordinary cluster of genitives,
       indicated by the number of apostrophes this final line contains.
       Why? One possible reason: this final stanza can be read as a
       prayer, full of longing for the return of Britain to the Catholic
       faith (look again at the closing stanzas of *The Loss of the
       Eurydice*, p. 40). Two controlling nouns in the final line are *fire*
       (midway) and *Lord* (at the very end), the last word of the whole
       poem. Can you think of ways of linking these terms together,
       given the various processes which fire can symbolize (warmth,
       life, destruction, Hell, etc.)?

Moonrise, June 19th 1879

The poet recounts an imaginatively significant experience in this
short, unfinished lyric. Is there a quality of a great and sudden
revelation in it as described by Hopkins? In a half-waking state he
witnesses an encounter between the all but transparent (female)
midsummer moon and the substantial, brooding (male) mass of
the nearby mountain. What do you think it is that makes the
experience *the prized, the desirable sight* (6)? Is this another instance
of Hopkins's capacity to evoke a perception of the natural world
and surround it with a deep sense of meaning and value? If this is
the case, can you think of other poems where something similar
occurs? Why do you think Hopkins left the poem incomplete?

3 **pairing of paradisaïcal fruit**   thin slice of plantain (Latin –
  musa paradisaica). Does the 'heavenly' adjective hint at another
  dimension to the text?
4 **Maenefa**   hill close to St Beuno's College in north Wales (see
  Chronology section).
5 **cusp**   sharp hooked end.
  fluke   sharp end piece of anchor.
  fanged   caught, trapped.

God's Grandeur

This poem is a sonnet, a literary form much used by Hopkins.
The sonnet originated in Italian writing of the thirteenth century,
but in English literature it became a commonly used and
developed form only in the Elizabethan period towards the close
of the sixteenth century. It is a form subject to rules or
conventions in terms of lines, rhyme schemes adopted, and
structure. The majority of the poems in this selection are
actually in sonnet form: fourteen lines of verse, divided in ratio
8:6, the former part called the octet, the latter the sestet. That
two-part structure is important; one of the conventions about
sonnets is that often the sestet concludes a line of thought
initiated in the octet. Hopkins uses only two rhymes throughout
the octets of his sonnets; they all rhyme *abba abba* (you can easily
test this for yourself!). There is more variety in the rhyming
schemes used in the sestets, though here again only two rhymes
are ever employed.

So, a poet whose preferred form is restricted to only four
rhyming sounds in fourteen lines. Why? You will probably come
up with your own ideas as you think further about Hopkins, but
here are some opening hypotheses:

1 He enjoyed setting himself difficult technical challenges.
2 He thought that restricting rhymes helped keep expression
  as economical as possible.

3 He considered that a small number of rhyming sounds makes a greater impact in aural terms.

(See the discussion of this text in Interpretations p. 143.)

1 **charged** as with an electrical current? Implicit in the metaphor is a sense of divine creative and sustaining energy. For other uses of electrical ideas, see *The Wreck of the Deutschland* (p. 27, 213), *The Loss of the Eurydice* (p. 37, 24) and its related Notes (p. 91), and Interpretations p. 159.

2 **like shining from shook foil** Hopkins's emphatic comment on this image in a letter to Robert Bridges is worth noting here:

I mean foil in its sense of leaf or tinsel, and no other word whatever will give the effect I want. Shaken goldfoil gives off broad glares like sheet lightning and also, and this is true of nothing else, owing to its zigzag dints and creasings and network of small many cornered facets, a sort of fork lightning too.
(Letter to Robert Bridges, 4 January 1883)

5 Why the three-fold repetition here? Is it effective?

6 **seared... bleared, smeared** The internal rhyme has a rhythmical function too, continued with the rhyme (*wears... shares*) in line 7.

12–14 **Oh... ah!** Such interjections are the stuff of lyric poetry, features of its emotional idiom. But it is worth noting how the second sound actually dislocates a phrase, perhaps making the end of the poem thereby more interesting.

The Starlight Night

This sonnet was written at the same time as *God's Grandeur*, March 1877. Exclamations litter the text, helping convey the tone of excitement, rapture and imaginative discovery. As with *God's Grandeur*, one way of thinking about the poem is to explore the relationship between octet and sestet, the former full of romantic visions of *fire-folk* (2), *diamond delves* (4), *elves'-eyes* (4), the latter explicitly signalling Christian concerns.

4 **delves**   obsolete word for 'mines'.
6 **whitebeam… abeles**   the former a tree with silvery white underleaves, the latter a white poplar.
8 **all a purchase, all is a prize**   a key line in this text; as a devout Catholic, Hopkins believed that Christ's death on the cross had saved mankind and nature from eternal damnation. The theme is fundamental to his awareness as a 'religious' poet.
10 **May-mess**   fruit tree blossom, a sign of spring.
11 **mealed-with-yellow sallows!**   invented compound term; pussy-willows (*sallows*) covered in a yellow, furry-textured flower.
13 **shocks**   stooks or sheaves (of corn).
piece-bright paling   a wooden wall through which starlight glints; a metaphor for the starry night sky.
14 **hallows**   saints (as in All Hallows: All Saints' Day).

'As kingfishers catch fire'

The sestet in this sonnet is restricted to a single rhyme (just like the octet of *The Windhover*, p. 34). Think about the octet–sestet relationship. Hopkins, like other poets, uses the sonnet as a device for expressing and clarifying thought. What kind of thinking is going on here?

Perhaps the crucial word in the poem is the first word of line 7: *Selves*. It is not, as you might think, a noun or prefix, as the word is characterized in most dictionaries. Instead it is a verb: 'to selve', which Hopkins coins for his own purposes, probably best paraphrased by the remainder of lines 7 and 8. You may find your feeling for this kind of reflection is developed by the sonnet *To what serves Mortal Beauty?* (p. 56).

1 the visual effect of the sun glinting off the bird and insect respectively.
3–4 **tucked**   is a version of 'plucked'; Hopkins concentrates on aural experience here just as line 1 focuses on vision. The description of the bells' echoing timbre has an onomatopoeic feel to it with the succession of rhymes and half-rhymes.

12–14 A basic theme here: God loves individuals to the extent that their lives try to imitate the perfection of Christ. As the kingfisher's perfection is physical, so a man's is moral and spiritual; each is thereby part of the perfect pattern of created nature.

Spring

There is again, in this sonnet, the tonal contrast between octet and sestet to think about: the one languid, a vision of paradise itself, the other more urgent. Paradise seems momentarily captured in an idyllic spring scene, only to be qualified by the framework of sin and salvation. Paradise, then the Fall; innocence, then experience; bliss, then sin, corruption, and death. It might be worth looking at the poem *Spring and Fall* (p. 46) for another expression of this perhaps idealized vision of the radiant (and temporary) innocence of youth.

3 **Thrush's... heavens**   greeny-blue, hence *little low heavens*.
4 **echoing timber**   of the trees, the wooden roof, or both?
6 **glassy**   enamelled, shining; suggesting a perfection of form associated more with paradise than with the everyday world?
10 **strain**   offspring, but also melody, song.
12 **cloud... and sour with sinning**   the *juice* (9) seen as a *strain of the earth's sweet being* (10), tainted by sin. Is Hopkins thinking of milk as the primal 'juice'?
14 **O maid's child**   Christ.

The Sea and the Skylark

This sonnet was written on holiday in Rhyl, North Wales, May 1877. The religious theme in the sestet is far more implicit, oblique, than in other sonnets in this selection. The timeless sound and rhythm embodied in the noises made by skylark and sea (octet) are contrasted with the *sordid turbid time* (10) of human society.

Hopkins's sensory awareness reveals itself constantly in the poems as in his prose (notebooks, journals, diaries). Here, the stress is auditory, the accent put on onomatopoeic devices to catch the contrasted sound-worlds of sea and skylark (look especially at, and listen to, lines 5–8). The following extract from a letter to Bridges written in 1882 says a good deal about this sound-world; it also gives you a flavour of the descriptive power of Hopkins the prose writer:

> The lark's song, which from his height gives the impression of something falling to the earth and not vertically quite but trickingly or wavingly, something as a skein of silk ribbed by having been tightly wound on a narrow card... The lark in wild glee races the reel round, paying or dealing out and down the turns of the skein...
>
> **(Letter to Robert Bridges, 26 November 1882)**

2 **Trench** As elsewhere, part of Hopkins's linguistic impact comes from his boldness in using coinages, verbal inventions. Here *Trench* is a verb, not a noun, meaning 'to make a deep impression'.

3 **With a flood or a fall** extremes of tidal conditions, but both words have deep theological resonances too; *flood* links to Noah and the Ark (Genesis 7), while *fall* echoes the myth of mankind's expulsion from the Garden of Eden (Genesis 3). Do you think a case might be made for this biblical aspect to the phrase as used here by Hopkins, particularly in the light of the ideas developed in the sestet? Or are any biblical echoes merely a coincidence?

9 **this shallow and frail town** Rhyl? The resort, located a few miles to the north of St Beuno's College, on the North Wales coast, was largely a by-product of the building of the Chester to Holyhead railway in the 1840s. It was a favourite haunt for holidaymakers from the industrial towns of nearby Lancashire.

10 **turbid** muddy, crowded.

12 **earth's past prime** another Garden of Eden allusion?

In the Valley of the Elwy

This is a curious sonnet because it seems to run counter to the tendency highlighted elsewhere for Hopkins's octets to establish a 'naturalist' context into which explicitly Christian motifs are introduced in the sestet. Here, the octet refers to the poet's happy memories of hospitality when he thought he did not deserve it. The start of the sestet probably leads you on to assume that this welcoming house was in Wales, in that very valley of the Elwy from which the sonnet gets its title. So lines 9–10 might be read as linking a hospitable Welsh home to the welcoming natural environment of Wales itself. But if this is so neatly the case, where does line 11 fit in? On this reading of the poem, isn't the *inmate* the kindly host who cared for the poet? Further mystification, with the outline of a possible solution, comes in a letter to Bridges where Hopkins writes:

> The kind people of the sonnet were the Watsons of Shooter's Hill, London, nothing to do with the Elwy... The frame of the sonnet is a rule of three sum wrong, thus: As the sweet smell to those kind people so the Welsh landscape is NOT to the Welsh; and then the author and principle of all four terms is asked to bring the sum right.
>
> (Letter to Robert Bridges, 8 April 1879)

This sonnet offers a valuable lesson about premature conclusions reached from misleading contextual clues! It also amply demonstrates the quirky, contrary nature of Hopkins's intellect – always ready to go off at a tangent or turn an expected line of thought inside out. You have been warned.

5 **cordial**   literally, something stimulating the heart – so, refreshing, warm, welcoming.
  made those kind people a hood   The air 'hoods' (covers and protects) the people.
9 **combes**   gentle valleys.

12–14   As in *The Sea and the Skylark* (p. 33), do we see Hopkins's sense
of the imperfect and evil state of mankind in nature breaking
through?

The Windhover

You may find it helpful to refer to the discussion of this poem in
Interpretations (pp. 127–31). The textual notes here are intended
to complement that discussion.

1   **morning's minion**   A *minion* is, literally, a favourite child or
servant, a king's favourite; the French origins of the word
(*mignon* meaning darling) link directly to *daylight's dauphin* (2).

2   **daylight's dauphin**   crown prince, heir to daylight.
dapple-dawn-drawn   attracted from his overnight resting
place by the light of dawn. Note the use of compounds for
both economy and impact.

4   **wimpling**   rippling, through effort and through effect of wind?

6   **bow-bend**   wide arc.

8   **achieve**   achievement; noun disguised as verb again, for
economy and impact?

9   **plume**   Note the proximity in the line to *pride*; peacock and
ostrich plumes are often associated with (human) display, or do
you think it more likely that Hopkins is still restricting his
thought to the falcon's own feathers?

10   **Buckle!**   crucial (and ambiguous) term; collapse, link together,
put on armour, give way to – all possible senses, none
obviously ruled out by this context. It is the imperative
(commanding) verb which controls the whole of the previous
line.

11   **chevalier**   knight, hero; like *minion* (1) and *dauphin* (2), a word
taken directly from French, and again the medieval, chivalric
colouring.

12   **sillion**   strip of land to be ploughed.

13   **blue-bleak**   *bleak* because, apparently, lifeless and cold?

14   **gall**   literally, injure, annoy or humiliate themselves; how can
embers be described as doing things they feel, physically or

emotionally, unless it is not just embers that these lines are concerned with?

gash gold-vermilion   are cut open to reveal rich colours (contrasted with *blue-bleak* 13), associated with the colours of royalty in heraldry. *Vermilion* may also have associations with the colour of blood. Some commentators have suggested that just as the start of the poem is set at dawn, so the image at the close is of dusk; how persuasive do you find this reading yourself?

Pied Beauty

Structurally, this poem is a curiosity. It is a 'curtal' sonnet, condensed or abbreviated into ten and a half lines rather than the usual fourteen. The initial octet is now a sestet and the closing sestet is now a quartet, with a final half-line or tailpiece. (See also *Peace* p. 44.)

In celebrating the heterogeneous, prolific character of the natural world, the poem has often been regarded as displaying Hopkins's voice and technique at their most characteristic. Why do you think editors of anthologies have so frequently preferred this poem against others in giving readers a sense of Hopkins's writing? For further discussion of this poem see Interpretations p. 143.

The word *Pied* in the title means 'Parti-coloured... also of three or more colours in patches or blotches' (*OED*).

2 **of couple-colour as a brinded cow**   variously coloured, like a 'brindled' cow.

4 **Fresh-firecoal chestnut-falls**   *Chestnuts as bright as coals or spots of vermilion*, an observation Hopkins made in his Journal (in September 1868) nearly a decade before writing this sonnet.

5 **fold, fallow, and plough**   referring respectively to grazing, fallow, and cultivated fields; 'mixed' farming giving the landscape the patchwork effect Hopkins notes and admires.

6 **trim**   dress, clothing.

7 **counter... spare**   unique... undecorated.
8 **freckled**   variegated.
10 **beauty past change**   the eternal, so immutable, beauty of the creator contrasted with the ever-changing variety evident in nature, the creation.

The Caged Skylark

This sonnet has a rather conventional premise: the wild bird trapped in a cage, a symbol for the eternal soul trapped in a mortal body. It is not, perhaps, made more interesting by any sense of the poet going off at tangents? Wild bird in cage: soul in body is an analogy, an extended comparison. Does Hopkins manage to sustain that analogy throughout the length of his sonnet or do you feel that instead the comparison breaks down before the end?

1 **scanted**   typically fertile invention; the sense something like 'existing in a mean and basic way'.
2 **bone-house**   rib-cage, body.
3 **fells**   moors.
12–14 an allusion to the Christian belief that the virtuous souls in Heaven will reassume their physical form after the Last Judgement.

Hurrahing in Harvest

This sonnet reveals an ecstatic awareness of nature enhanced and intensified by awareness of the divine being who creates and sustains. Hopkins describes it, in a letter to Bridges of July 1878, as: *the outcome of half an hour of extreme enthusiasm as I walked home alone one day from fishing in the Elwy*. The emphatic alliterations of lines 1–4 certainly evoke something at once sensuous and intoxicated (*extreme enthusiasm?*).

  1 **barbarous** wild
  6 **glean** a pun; 'gleaning' is part of the cleaning-up process after the harvest and also a word for 'glimpsing'.
11–12 These lines form the religious nucleus of this text; physical, inanimate nature is informed by the divine, the poet's joy in nature's beauty is virtually interchangeable with his joy at being in the presence of God.
  13 **The heart rears wings** a complex image. Do you think here of the windhover, of the Holy Spirit symbolized as the dove of peace? Is the sense less prescriptive or specific than either of these?

The Loss of the Eurydice

A shorter sea narrative than *The Wreck of the Deutschland*, but again a text in which Hopkins tries to integrate elements of dramatic narrative and religious reflection.

Hopkins took the 'musical' dimensions of this text – its aural impact when read aloud correctly – very seriously, as this remark in a letter to Bridges indicates:

> To do the *Eurydice* any kind of justice you must not slovenly read it with the eyes but with your ears, as if the paper were declaiming it at you. For instance the line 'she had come from a cruise, training seamen' read without proper stress and declaim is mere Lloyd's Shipping Intelligence; properly read it is quite a different thing. Stress is the life of it.
>
> **(Letter to Robert Bridges, 13 May 1878)**

This concern for the musical aspect, the effect on us as listeners rather than readers, often figures in Hopkins's written comments on his work (see for example the Notes to the later sonnets *Harry Ploughman* (p. 114) and *Tom's Garland* (p. 115), and Interpretations pp. 145–46).

Some historical details may help to establish the context of Hopkins's narrative. The *Eurydice* was a naval training ship which foundered off the Isle of Wight in March 1878 as it returned from a voyage to the West Indies. Unlike the *Deutschland*, there were no persecuted German nuns on board to provoke Hopkins's sense of awe and outrage, but the text does suggest that he was inspired by the loss of so many young sailors to create this dramatic reflection on life and death.

The poem falls into two fairly distinct parts. Stanzas 1–21 focus largely on the events leading up to and surrounding the capsize of the ship in a severe storm. The captain, Marcus Hare, is singled out, as is one Sydney Fletcher, who through *a lifebelt and God's will* (63) survived the sinking and was rescued by another vessel. The final three stanzas of this first part focus quite explicitly on the corpse of a young sailor, *of lovely manly mould* (74), and on Hopkins's sense of loss at his beauty and talent wasted.

By contrast, stanzas 22–30, like the final section of *The Wreck of the Deutschland*, shift attention from the watery drama to attempt a link between a local tragedy and a national, historical one. Your own thoughts about the success or otherwise of the poem may well hinge on whether you find this imaginative leap convincing. Hopkins is thinking back to the pre-Reformation era when Roman Catholicism was the mode of Christianity practised in Britain. For Hopkins, the devout convert and Jesuit priest, this was the only authentic and true form of Christian witness. He is reflecting on the fact that those who drowned in the *Eurydice* died unabsolved, that is not in a state of grace before God.

As in the longer poem, many of the challenges Hopkins sets us as readers are caused by his compressed idiom; it is up to you to decide whether the effort of wrestling with those challenges is finally justified.

1 **concerned thee** ambiguous? meaning 'mattered to you' or 'was your responsibility'; significant this early in the poem.
5–6 **One... oak!** a dramatic pun; *hearts of oak* equals sailors, cut down like a mighty oak by a powerful lightning bolt.
7 **flockbells** a Hopkins coinage; the bells on sheep grazing on the steep seaward facing slopes (*forefalls* 8 another invention).

12 **lade**   a contraction rather than an invention; more expected would be 'lading' meaning 'cargo'.

16 **bole and bloom**   a nicely alliterative phrase: trunk and foliage, the whole tree.

23 **Boreas**   north wind (from Greek mythology).

24 **deadly-electric**   vivid, curiously modern-sounding phrase, referring to the lightning storm. Readers have found the intended rhyme in lines 23–4 (*he/Came... electric*, the hard C of *Came* rhyming with the *ic* of *electric*) very perverse and forced; what is your view?

27–8 **Hailropes... Heavengravel**   from the perverse to the inspired? Aggressive sounding coinages for foul weather.

29–32 **Carisbrook... Appledurcombe... Ventnor... Boniface Down**   places on the Isle of Wight, familiar to Hopkins from holidays.

34 **royals**   sails used in fine weather. Is there the hint of something reckless about the conduct of the ship as it is about to meet severe weather?

40 **messes of mortals**   alliteration plus a pun ('mess' as in ship's mess; also as in untidy heap, or even human excrement, waste?).

43 **she**   the ship; what had protected the men from the sea is now their tomb.

47 **Cheer's death**   despair.

48 **champ-white**   why *champ*?

50 **Right, rude of feature...**   paraphrase as 'Right – duty, the voice of conscience – is thought to say to the captain...'

53–6 Is this stanza made opaque in meaning by fussy syntax? It isn't helped by the feeling that the actual thought here, paraphrased by Hopkins in a letter to Bridges in May 1878 as: *even those who seem unconscientious will act the right part at a great push*, seems at a tangent to the direction of the narrative.

68 **rivelling**   causing to wrinkle.

77 **how all things suit!**   beauty as the absolute symmetry or agreement of constituent parts. This idea is very important to Hopkins, and the essence of his own aesthetic throughout his poetry. (See Interpretations pp. 151–53.)

85 **He was but one... more**   the transition point to the wider historical reflection developed in the final nine stanzas.

89 **bygones**   the Reformation, the dissolution of the monasteries,

etc. in the sixteenth century, when Henry VIII broke the links between the Christian faith in England and the traditional authority of the Pope in Rome.

92 **hoar-hallowed shrines unvisited**   shrines, places of pilgrimage, made holy through their very age (*hoar*). Note the richness of the vowel sounds here.

94 **wildworth**   wild flowers; a metaphor for the sailors, now *blown*.

95–6 **in / Unchrist**   a striking phrase; the sailors are damned because they were raised in a country (Britain) Hopkins sees as having turned its back on God (*all rolled in ruin*).

98 **Wondering… it**   This opens up a huge theological speculation; if the Reformation was so complete a tragedy for the British people, why did God allow it to happen?

101 **a starlight-wender**   a nocturnal traveller, a medieval pilgrim, guided by the stars towards the shrine which is the goal of his journey.

102 **Walsingham Way**   the pilgrims' way to Walsingham, the north Norfolk shrine to the Virgin Mary.

117–20 **Not that hell… pity-eternal**   It might be worth thinking about the tone or tones with which this poem ends and comparing them with the ending of *The Wreck of the Deutschland*. The thought here is part of Catholic eschatology as Hopkins understood it: the Catholic doctrine of salvation. Until the Last Judgement itself, the fate of those who die outside the state of grace will remain undecided; this should encourage their relatives and loved ones to continue praying for their salvation as divine pity may yet be stirred.

Duns Scotus's Oxford

The Duns Scotus of this sonnet was a medieval Catholic philosopher, a vital formative influence on the mind of Hopkins after his conversion to Catholicism. The basics of that influence are looked at in the Interpretations (p. 152). He is supposed to have lectured in Oxford sometime at the start of the fourteenth century. The sonnet can be viewed as a well-crafted piece of intellectual and spiritual hero-worship: *this air I gather and I release/He lived on*; (9–10).

The octet provides Hopkins with the chance to create a description of the Oxford he himself knew well. It also allows him to attack the (sub)urban sprawl of the expanding city of the 1870s, the *graceless growth* (7) interposing itself between the ancient collegiate centre and the beauties of the surrounding countryside.

4 **coped**   matched (their power).
5 **sours**   Hopkins notes in a letter of February 1879, *that landscape, the charm of Oxford, green shouldering grey, which is already abridged and soured.*
12 **realty**   realism. The phrase used here underlines Hopkins's admiration for Duns Scotus as a metaphysician, a philosopher interested in the nature of existence and being itself.
14   The reference here is to a famous theological debate in Paris, where Hopkins's hero successfully defended the doctrine of the Immaculate Conception, the belief that Mary the mother of Christ was the only human to be born without the stain of original sin (*without spot*). The doctrine was an article of Catholic faith in which Hopkins had a fierce belief.

Binsey Poplars

A lyric constructed in three eight-line stanzas. The feeling informing the text seems distinctly contemporary. Can you find any other evidence in this selection of Hopkins's 'green' credentials? For further discussion of this poem see Interpretations pp. 147–48.

1 **aspens**   broad-leaved poplars.
10 **delve or hew**   dig or chop down.
12–15   A dramatic image; nature's integrity vulnerable as eyesight itself.
19 **After-comers**   posterity; but an obsolete term, deliberately revived here by Hopkins. Why?

21 **unselve** disintegration/destruction of the scene's unique, particular identity. (On *Selves*, see Note to line 7 of 'As *kingfishers catch fire*' p. 82).

22–4 The repetition is curious, as if Hopkins wishes to stress the pathos of the destruction by repeating this tender-sounding phrase. The word *especial* has particular force in Hopkins's mind; it is associated with 'selve' and **inscape** (see Interpretations pp. 151–53) as a term referring to the unique and unrepeatable quality in our experience of phenomena. See also line 2 of *Henry Purcell* (p. 43), probably written at about the same time, during Hopkins's short period of parish work in Oxford. Another possible explanation of the marked repetitions at the end of this text is that Hopkins may have been thinking of a musical setting for the poem. None of these explanations excludes the others.

Henry Purcell

Henry Purcell (1659–95) is generally regarded as the greatest English composer of the seventeenth century. The veneration felt by Hopkins is doubly evident here, with the prose dedication to Purcell's *divine genius* prefacing the sonnet itself.

It is only fair to add that whereas Hopkins's feeling for the philosopher, Duns Scotus, is expressed in a comparatively direct manner, the initial impression any reader will have of the Purcell sonnet is of a tortuous, cryptic puzzle. Part of the challenge comes from the (simple) fact that Hopkins saw the sonnet in general as a vehicle for thought; complex thoughts conveyed within the restrictive terms of a sonnet are likely to emerge looking even more complex. This compacting tendency gets more pronounced in Hopkins's later sonnets, but is just as much a feature here.

Some indication of the problem is offered by the paraphrase of the sonnet which Hopkins provided in a letter to Bridges of January 1883; it is worth quoting, not only for the light it may shed on this sonnet, but also as an example of the clarity which often distinguishes Hopkins's prose. Additionally, the fact that Hopkins realized, to his dismay, that even his most ardent readers found barriers to understanding may give you comfort in your own engagements with these poems!

> The sonnet on Purcell means this: 1–4. I hope Purcell is not damned for being a Protestant, because I love his genius. 5–8. And that not so much for gifts he shares, even though it shd. be in higher measure, with other musicians as for his own individuality. 9–14. So that while he is aiming only at impressing me his hearer with the meaning in hand I am looking out meanwhile for his specific, his individual markings and mottlings, 'the sakes of him'. It is as when a bird thinking only of soaring spreads its wings: a beholder may happen then to have his attention drawn by the act to the plumage displayed. In particular, the first lines mean: May Purcell, O may he have died a good death and that soul which I love so much and which breathes or stirs so unmistakeably in his works have parted from the body and passed away... It is somewhat dismaying to find I am so unintelligible though, especially in one of my very best pieces.
>
> **(Letter to Robert Bridges, 4 January 1883)**

6 **nursle** foster, care for.

8 **self** key term; when he listens to Purcell's music, Hopkins experiences his **inscape**, the unique and particular identity which distinguishes Purcell and his genius from all other men (and all other geniuses).

9 **lift me, lay me!** a kind of hopeful prayer; may the angelic music inspire and/or soothe me!

10 **sakes** In the same letter to Bridges as quoted above, Hopkins remarks, *'Sakes' is hazardous: about that point I was more bent on saying my say than on being understood in it.* In any consideration of Hopkins's difficulty, that remark is worth recalling; comprehension in a reader is seen as secondary to precise expression of an image or perception. For Hopkins, a thing's 'sake' is that which most distinguishes it outside its physical form, so for a human genius, the 'sake' would be that aspect of

genius for which the individual is celebrated, so for Purcell, his music.

quaint moonmarks   *I was thinking of a bird's quill feathers*, Hopkins remarks in same letter as above.

13 **wuthering**   noise and rush of wind. (Compare with *Wuthering Heights*.)

14 **but** only, merely.

Peace

Like *Pied Beauty* (p. 35), this is a 'curtal' sonnet. Note how the rhyme scheme links together the two structures of the sonnet. Rhythmically, the use of repetitions and the series of rhetorical questions addressed to Peace give the first part of the poem a restless, even nervous quality. The effect, by design, is anything but peaceful! This dissonance between style and subject matter may offer a useful starting point for discussion of the text.

7 **reaving**   robbing, plundering.

9 **plumes to Peace thereafter**   *plumes* continues the bird metaphor set up in the opening six lines; the sense is of a fledgling (*Patience* 8) maturing into the splendour of the adult bird (Peace itself).

Felix Randal

In this sonnet links between life and poetry seem especially intimate; a poem arising directly from Hopkins's experience of life and death among the working-class poor of Liverpool as a parish priest.

On one level, this is a poem about the death of a once strong and healthy man, a man dependent on physical strength in his working life, and the way that death appears to the priest who had comforted him in his final illness. But alongside that narrative other elements appear: Hopkins's acute sense of physical beauty and prowess; the relationship between physical distress and spiritual relief; the strong feeling of mortality emerging at the close of the poem. One way into this text is to think about it as an elegy: a poem of mourning for the dead, for a fellow man whose **inscape** Hopkins admired for very different reasons to the inscapes celebrated in his sonnets on Henry Purcell and Duns Scotus.

1 **farrier**   person working in a smithy making and fitting horse-shoes.
   O is he dead then?   Why do you think Hopkins uses the present tense question form here?

6 **anointed**   given the last rites, a sacrament reserved for those gravely ill or close to death.

7 **sweet reprieve and ransom**   Holy Communion; the re-enactment of the sacrifice through which Christ on the cross reconciled God and man.

8 **all road ever**   Lancashire dialect form for 'however' used deliberately in a Lancashire context: the farrier was a member of Hopkins's Liverpool parish.

13 **random**   (architecture) composed of rough, irregular stones.
   grim   grimy (dialect).

14 **sandal!**   archaic term for type of horse-shoe, rather than a convenient rhyme for *Randal!* It is worth noting here that the farrier's surname is a pseudonym, the actual name was Spencer, but the forename is identical. *Felix* is a Latin word, meaning 'lucky' or 'fortunate'; appropriate or ironic in the case of the farrier of Hopkins's sonnet?

Spring and Fall

Notice the dedication, *to a Young Child*, the *Margaret* addressed right from the start of the opening line. If you have a strong feeling for this poem, the factors behind that feeling may be as follows: the directness of form, the easy fluency of the rhythm and the accessibility of images and language serve to heighten the feeling that Hopkins is dealing with a great theme here, all too glibly summarized by a term like 'innocence and experience'. How do you react to the thought that the poem has a direct appeal missing from at least some of the sonnets with their precise and complex lines of argument? For further discussion of this poem see Interpretations p. 151.

2 **unleaving** a neat invention; what trees do in the autumn.
8 **worlds of wanwood leafmeal lie** The alliteration helps stress an evocative image, which risks being shattered if analysed too literally. The young girl is upset (*grieving* 1), by the first signs of autumn in a wood; her older, more experienced self will have so many other elements of transience or mutability to grieve over that she will not be touched again by autumn and its changes, even on the grandest scale.
13 **ghost** soul, spirit.
14 **blight** of original sin?

Inversnaid

Three stanzas of intense verbal description, followed by a flat, generalized conclusion; a fair response to the poem, or do you think there is more to the relationship between the parts than this suggests? For further discussion see Interpretations pp. 149–50.

3 **coop... comb** water enclosed (as in a rock pool); water freely moving.
4 **Flutes** architectural expression for 'ridges', applied here not to stonework but to water channelled between rocks by a strong current.
6 **twindles** Lancashire dialect word for 'twins', but also perhaps a Hopkins invention, combining 'twins' and 'spindles'?
9 **Degged** Lancashire term again meaning 'sprinkled'. (See *Felix Randal* p. 45, 8 for other use of Lancashire dialect.)
11 **heathpacks** heather.

flitches of fern   like thin cuts from a tree trunk.
12 **beadbonny ash**   mountain ash, full of autumn berries (an apt use of the Scots *bonny* here, for the Scottish context).

The Leaden Echo and the Golden Echo

Some background information might be helpful here. Hopkins first came across the legend of St Winefred while studying for the Catholic priesthood at St Beuno's College in North Wales. He was attracted to the legend and to the well at Holywell named after the saint. He planned a verse drama on the legend, but although some fragments (such as this song) were written, he never completed the project. The legend itself is about chastity and martyrdom, religious concepts with which Hopkins is often preoccupied. Winefred, daughter of a seventh-century Welsh lord, and niece of St Beuno, decides to dedicate her virginity to God. Prince Caradoc becomes obsessed by her beauty; she spurns him and enraged by such rejection he cuts off her head with his sword. A well springs up where the head falls to the ground. In some versions St Beuno brings his niece back to life and his curse then dispatches Caradoc to damnation.

It makes sense to assume that Hopkins composed this 'Maidens' song' with a musical setting in mind, and with two contrasted voices or voice groups, the one 'leaden', the other 'golden'. All of this suggests an antiphonal setting, with the contrasts in mood in the two echoes underlined by a musical treatment exploiting the opportunities the text offers for word-painting and dramatic oppositions.

The Leaden Echo

1 Hopkins's remarks on this beginning, in a letter to Bridges of November 1882, throw considerable light on what kind of effects and mood he was trying to establish in this poem:

99

> I cannot satisfy myself about the first line. You must know that words like 'charm' and 'enchantment' will not do: the thought is of beauty as something that can be physically kept and lost and by physical things only, like keys: then the things must come from the 'mundus muliebris' the world of women; and thirdly they must not be markedly old-fashioned. You will see that this limits the choice of words very much indeed… 'Back' is not pretty, but it gives that feeling of physical constraint which I want.
>
> **(Letter to Robert Bridges, 4 November 1882)**

8 **wisdom is early to despair** the wise despair first, since they are the first to see how transient beauty is.

The Golden Echo

1 **Spare!** rhyme picked up from the six-fold repetition of *despair* (15–16) at the close of *The Leaden Echo*. Is the exclamation itself used to signal a dramatic change in mood here?

9 **dangerously** the idea of physical beauty as both aesthetically compelling and morally corrupting, a theme to which Hopkins often returns (see comments in the Notes to the late sonnet *To what serves Mortal Beauty?*, pp. 105–07).

26 **fagged** worn out.
fashed (Scots term) careworn.
cogged old word for deceived, betrayed.

27 **the thing** physical beauty itself; lines 27–30 involve reference to the Catholic doctrine of the Resurrection, the existence of the redeemed after the Last Judgement will involve a perfection of their physical form as well as their souls.

Ribblesdale

Hopkins suggested this sonnet was a companion to *In the Valley of the Elwy*, p. 33. He also commented in a letter that *it is to be read very pausingly…* How do you think the theme or subject matter you find here goes along with this *very pausingly* idea?

One manuscript version of the poem is prefaced by the words of St Paul in Romans 8:19–20, a passage concerned with the effects on nature of the morally fallen and corrupt state of mankind. So, nature troubled by the Fall, a poem to be *read very pausingly*, a title referring to a wild part of the Lancashire landscape which Hopkins grew to admire. As so often in Hopkins's sonnets, the sestet develops an explicitly human focus where the octet stays nearer to 'natural' expectations encouraged by the sonnet's title.

- 1 **throng** meant here as an adjective, a Lancashire dialect word again, meaning 'crowded'.
- 2 **louched** dialect, meaning 'slouched', but maybe better suited to the sound patterns of line 2 with *l* sounds stressed in *low* and *appeal*.
- 10 **heir** links with Genesis 1:26–30, humanity *given dominion over the whole earth*; echoing the 'ecological' Hopkins of *Binsey Poplars*?
- 11 **selfbent** absorbed by selfish desires.
- 12 **reave** rob, plunder (as in *Peace*, p. 44, 7).
- 13–14 human indifference making the earth troubled, pre-occupied (*brows of such care*).

The Blessed Virgin compared to the Air we Breathe

The first things you might notice about this poem, besides its very explicit, explanatory-looking title, are its length and its rhythmical character. At 126 lines it is the third longest poem in this selection, structurally very different from the closely crafted sonnet form to which Hopkins so often returns. And rhythmically, the short line, technically iambic trimeter, giving three feet to the line in a mixture of rhyming couplets and triplets, gives a brisk, clipped effect, again contrasted with the complex rhythms and counter-rhythms found elsewhere in this selection.

These departures from Hopkins's norms may be partly

explained by the circumstances surrounding the poem's composition. In 1883 Hopkins was teaching at Stonyhurst, the Jesuit seminary in Lancashire. It was a custom at the college for poems in honour of the Virgin Mary to be displayed before her statue during May, her month in the Church calendar. This custom provided the immediate stimulus for the poem.

5 **-flixed** from 'flix', a kind of animal fur.

24 **Mary Immaculate** the doctrine that Mary the mother of Christ alone among mankind was born without stain of original sin.

27 **Great as no goddess's** contrasting true religion from the myths of pre-Christian cultures.

39 **Mantles** covers and protects, as under a 'mantle', a woman's loose cloak.

42 **almoner** one responsible for dispensing alms, charity for the poor. Hopkins goes on to say that Mary is less the dispenser of charity from God to man than one form of that divine charity itself.

48 **ghostly** as often, spiritual.

60 **Nazareths** linked to *Bethlems* (63, 65); Christ was conceived in Nazareth and born in a stable in Bethlehem.

73–126 Possibly the most rewarding facet of the text for readers whose sympathies may not be greatly stirred by the Catholic doctrine of the Virgin. Between lines 73 and 113 Hopkins develops an ambitious analogy, both scientific and imaginative. As the sun's impact is mediated by the earth's atmosphere, producing refracted light that allows us to see the rich blue of the sky, so Hopkins suggests here that Mary is the *atmosphere* (115) mediating between imperfect humans and the unbearable majesty of God. Even if you are unmoved by the theology, the image integrates the physical universe, human perception, and Hopkins's sense of the presence of God.

80 **Charged** again the use of a word with electrical, energy-filled associations (look back at its use in the sonnet *God's Grandeur*, p. 31).

101 **Quartz-fret** a gem cut so as to allow many piercing light points to show.

117 **wend**   journey, travel (see *The Loss of the Eurydice*, p. 40, 101).
126 The alliterations stress the theme contained in the key epithet
     world-mothering air (1, 124); according to the 'Marian' doctrine
     in which Hopkins believed, Mary was the mother of all
     mankind, not of Christ alone, and so the one perfect, morally
     pure woman to whom all might turn for spiritual comfort.

'To seem the stranger'

Counted among the so-called 'Sonnets of Desolation' (see
Interpretations p. 163). The theme, announced in line 1, is
Hopkins's experience of estrangement: homesick for England,
doing a job he finds uncongenial and exhausting, spiritually
troubled by the sense that he can no longer communicate with
God, the sonnet becomes a medium for exploring the poet's
distress and the factors behind it.

   2 **Father and mother dear**   Remember that Hopkins came from
      a prosperous middle-class family, strongly Anglican in their
      religion. The poet's conversion to Catholicism and decision to
      become a Catholic priest must have created real dilemmas of
      understanding and acceptance for them.
   4 **he my peace/my parting**   *he* is Christ; Hopkins's experience
      of belief is not one of reassurance but of 'the long night of the
      soul', distress and insecurity.
   8 **wars**   the contemporary Irish struggle for political freedom
      from Britain; Hopkins saw the legitimacy of that struggle,
      recognizing that he was in an unhappy and turbulent country.
9–10 **third/Remove**   Isolated by a three-fold exile: from parents,
      country, and an audience appreciative of his poetic powers.
11–14 The reference is to difficulties over prayer: Hopkins feels
      unable to pray, doubtful about whether those prayers he does
      manage ever reach their intended audience. This sharpens the
      sense of spiritual dejection.

'I wake and feel'

Another of the 'Sonnets of Desolation'. As before, the focus of distress is on the inability to communicate effectively with God, the spiritual pain now aggravated by insomnia and nightmares. Indeed, the sestet ends on a note of real despair; Hopkins likens his torment to that of the damned souls in Hell.

  1 **fell**   blow, but also the idea of an animal pelt, savage and alien.
  2 **we**   Hopkins talking to his *heart* (3) as a fellow-sufferer.
  7 **like dead letters sent**   an evocative simile, because it is so everyday; Hopkins feels like the lover whose letters are sent to the 'dead letter office' because his beloved has moved away and correspondence cannot be forwarded.
9–11 **I am gall... the curse**   The image behind the first triplet in this sestet is of the poet as a pain made concrete or material; he doesn't *feel* agony as something that might go away as it came, he *is* agony, a flesh and blood version of the experience itself.
  12 **Selfyeast**   human personality like a bread whose quality depends on the yeast (*spirit*) which causes dull ingredients like flour and water to become nourishing; the stress on 'self' is crucial in a poem full of self-disgust. For further discussion of this poem see Interpretations pp. 163–65.

'No worst'

Whereas the sense of distress in the previous two poems involves exploration of the poet's own agitated mental state, here a new element of questioning appears alongside that introspection. If the God in whom Hopkins believes is a God of love, why is the poet allowed to suffer so keenly? The sestet goes on to examine further the mental torment Hopkins is enduring, the imagery evoking vertigo. The symptoms depicted are so extreme that the stark ending hardly comes as a surprise; even so, the suicidal hints retain a strong sense of shock, coming as they do from a priest whose faith placed suicide among the most terrible of all sins. For further discussion of the poem see *Interpretations* pp. 163–65.

1 **No worst, there is none**   Notice the abrupt beginning, as if we are in the middle of an intimate conversation (compare with *Felix Randal*, p. 45). What is the effect of saying *worst* here rather than 'worse'?
pitched   two senses; thrown, but also tuning a stringed instrument.

2 **forepangs**   previous pains.

3 **Comforter**   the Holy Spirit.

5 **herds-long**   strong metaphor; with *heave* suggesting cries of pain produced only with great effort, we can imagine here the moans of cattle in distress, dumb and incapable of finding any remedy for their suffering.

7–8 **'ling-/Ering!'**   Does the stretched-out effect of the line-break perhaps suggest a black kind of word-play?

8 **fell**   the adjective 'deadly', not the noun form as in the opening line of '*I wake and feel*' (p. 55).
force   contraction of 'perforce', necessarily.

9 **mind, mind**   probably a simple repetition of the noun, although the second *mind* may also have the sense 'look', 'note'.
fall   the vertigo idea; the sound is a deliberate echo in half-rhyme of *fell* in the preceding line.

12 **Durance**   another contraction, of 'endurance'.

13 **a comfort**   the idea developed in the final line; *death*, or its temporary version, *sleep*, puts an end to mental suffering, though remember the sense of insomnia suggested in '*I wake and feel*'.

To what serves Mortal Beauty?

The ideas in this sonnet explore some of Hopkins's most serious preoccupations. The question giving the sonnet its title and driving force was bound to be one especially urgent to a mind

such as Hopkins's; with such intense apprehension of the
beautiful in nature, including fellow human beings, coupled to
belief in an all-powerful and judging God, it was inevitable that
Hopkins felt the need to argue out the relationship proper
between full awareness of natural beauty and obedience to God.
Remarks in a letter written to Robert Bridges in 1879, almost six
years earlier, offer a useful gloss:

> I think then no one can admire beauty of the body more than I
> do, and it is of course a comfort to find beauty in a friend or a
> friend in beauty. But this kind of beauty is dangerous. Then
> comes beauty of the mind, such as genius, and this is greater
> than beauty of the body and not to call dangerous. And more
> beautiful than the beauty of the mind is beauty of character,
> the 'handsome heart'.
>
> (Letter to Robert Bridges, 1879)

Physical beauty can be *dangerous* (1) because it offers temptation,
arousing the passions. Such loss of rational control, giving way
to instinctive behaviour, is the spiritual opposite to the life most
desired by the believer, living by grace, resisting temptation to
sin. More than that, Hopkins believed that *mortal beauty* (1) could
itself bring about the death of the soul. Note that the adjective
Mortal in the title has more than one sense: not only 'something
that will die', but also 'deadly', 'causing death'.

The thought-process in this closely-reasoned poem
approximates to this: beauty can be dangerous, exciting the
passion; but, so long as its perception is a means to an end, and
not a sensual end in itself, such beauty can be instructive; the
example of Pope Gregory (see Note to line 7); it is right to love
the beauty of fellow humans, as the most complete *mortal beauty*
(1) created by God; but the correct way to cope with such beauty,
potentially corrupting, is to see it for what it is, one kind of
evidence for divine power and goodness, of an inferior kind; by
contrast, divine grace itself offers the most complete beauty of
all, the only beauty we might beneficially aim to possess.

2 **O-seal-that-so | feature**   a face so perfect we might want to preserve it from any subsequent change.

3 **Purcell tune**   See Notes to *Henry Purcell* sonnet (pp. 94–6).

4–5 **glance... gaze**   difference between the two important for the argument developed here.

7 **Gregory**   Pope Gregory (*c.* AD 600). The story is that seeing Britons on sale in a Roman market Gregory exclaimed *Non Angli, sed Angeli* ('They're angels, not Britons!'). Seeing these *Angli* inspired him to send St Augustine (of Canterbury) on a mission to convert England to Christianity.

8 **that day's dear chance**   The conversion of England apparently traced back to a lucky accident.

11 **Self flashes off frame and face**   Self is most readily perceived in appearance? So human beauty is closest to divine beauty in nature? *Self* links directly to the individual's **inscape.** (see Interpretations pp. 151–54.)

12 **own**   acknowledge, admit (read with *heaven's sweet gift* 13).

14 Would that those you recognize as beautiful might yet achieve that highest condition of beauty, the spiritual beauty given by divine grace? Is this line itself a kind of prayer, apt culmination for a Jesuit's reflections on beauty, sin and salvation?

(The Soldier)

Here, as elsewhere, the title is bracketed simply because Hopkins left the poem without a title; the brackets indicate the title is the work of his first editor, Robert Bridges.

The opening suggests conversation or discussion; it's as if we are overhearing an exchange of (maybe differing) views or even eavesdropping on someone's train of thought. The actual thought process is provocative and involved. Why do people seeing soldiers handsomely turned out in dress uniform *bless* them? Hopkins finds an answer in the idea that because the *calling* is *manly* (4), people hope or imagine that the individuals wearing the uniform are themselves as morally excellent as their appearance is handsome. A connection is assumed between the moral and the aesthetic, between the category of conscience and conduct and that of beauty. That might catch some of the thinking in the octet. What happens subsequently in the sestet that concludes the sonnet? Is Hopkins saying that all soldiers are Christ-like? That Christ is the greatest of soldiers? That Christ is especially favourable towards the military? Or are we taken in an altogether different, even subversive, direction – only obliquely related to the theme of the first eight lines? If you look back to the sonnet *'As kingfishers catch fire...'* you might find a line of thought to compare with the ideas emerging in the latter part of this sonnet.

1 **seeing of a soldier** implies 'we look no further than the obvious symbolism of the uniform'.

2 **tars** sailors; the opening thought covers all fighting men, here clearly the soldiers and sailors defending the British Empire.

3 **clay** a religious metaphor at least as old as the creation myths of the Book of Genesis (in particular, chapter 2).

5 **makesbelieve** a telling word; it might suggest that the links we make between military splendour and moral excellence are illusory, even childish.

6 **deems** judges.
   dears... after values... as.

7 **sterling... smart** the moral/aesthetic contrast Hopkins builds throughout the octet.

9 Here the imagery of Christ the King as a mighty warrior vanquishing the powers of evil is tied up with the imagery of the Apocalypse, the catastrophic destruction of the world at the end of time, as narrated in the Book of Revelation. There is also a reference to Christ as the hero whose unequalled courage involves great deeds done in isolation, on behalf of others (compare the sentiment in a sermon written by Hopkins: 'he (Christ) led the way, went before his troops, was himself the vanguard, was the forlorn hope, bore the brunt of battle alone...').

13 **so-God-made-flesh does too** Christ, God become human, in the miracle of the incarnation.

(Carrion Comfort)

For the brackets around the title, see the notes for 'The Soldier'.

The starting point of the sonnet is a dialogue with *Despair* (1), one of the seven deadly sins, which Hopkins sees as offering him an easy but fatal release from his spiritual turmoil. Again perhaps there are the suicidal implications suggested at the end of 'No worst'. The difference is that this poem begins, with its four-fold repetition of the defiant *Not*, in a more vigorous mood of rejection. Despair is the terminal state of hopelessness, what remains when belief has disappeared. Hopkins insists that belief remains, however difficult it has become since God has chosen to test the poet by withdrawing from him. For us as readers the relationship between octet and sestet presents the real challenges of interpretation here. For further discussion of this poem see Interpretations pp. 165–66.

1 **carrion comfort** *carrion* is decaying/loathsome flesh; *comfort* consolation or food. The phrase, describing *Despair*, can be read as both 'comfort to carrion' and 'deriving comfort from carrion'.

4 **not choose not to be** deny the attraction of death and oblivion. *Not* is employed six times in four lines; is Hopkins maybe protesting too much here, as if what he strenuously denies might just have more of a grip on him than he dares admit?

5 **rude** adverb; rudely, brutally.

6 **wring-earth** characteristic invention, a strong compound adjective suggesting the world-shaking force of the power that assaults Hopkins.
   rock verb, going with *wouldst* (5).

9 **Why?** key word; why is despair so concerned to claim the poet's soul? The octet has graphically described the attacks of despair, and the questions have a real theological edge; why is God allowing the poet to be so tempted? In the sestet Hopkins attempts a coherent answer, a way of justifying God's refusal to intervene. You need to decide for yourself how effective that answer is, and how well it works with the ideas of the octet.

10 **coil** tumult, uproar.
   kissed the rod biblical image of submission to divine
   punishment and correction; despite his submission, Hopkins
   has felt no relief from torment. The image of the divine *rod*
   also figures in the sonnet *God's Grandeur*, (p. 31, 4) as well as in
   The Wreck of the Deutschland (p. 18, 10).
12 **hero** Christ?
14 **(my God!)** the believer's shock at realizing that his struggle is
   with God himself; the wrestling, struggling motif has strong
   echoes of the Old Testament, in particular Genesis 32, where
   Jacob wrestles with the angel.

'Patience, hard thing'

Look again at the earlier curtal sonnet, *Peace* (p. 44), where
Hopkins develops the idea of *Patience exquisite* (8) as the
precursor, the forerunner, of Peace itself. In the context of these
'Sonnets of Desolation' the decision to focus here on patience –
endurance, readiness to wait and suffer (the Latin verb *patior*
contains both senses) – is significant. In one of his devotional
writings, the *Comments on the Spiritual Exercises of St Ignatius
Loyola*, Hopkins advises: *Let him who is in desolation strive to
remain in patience, which is the virtue contrary to the troubles which
harass him; and let him think that he will shortly be consoled, making
diligent efforts against the desolation.* The octet develops the idea
that patience is itself the result of suffering or misfortune, while
the sestet suggests that for human *hearts* (9) to accommodate
themselves to God's will demands a readiness to suffer pain.
Whether the thoughts explored in the sonnet are convincing,
whether they articulate an experience Hopkins had now at last
actually felt, or was something he still desperately longed for, this
is for you to decide yourself. Certainly the tone offers a marked
contrast to the blackness evoked by several of the previous
sonnets.

1–4 Someone who asks for patience is also implicitly taking on the spiritual pain and discomfort it entails.

6 **No-where** *Rare patience* (5) is associated exclusively with want, misfortune, suffering.
ivy the metaphor is visually striking; capacity to endure masks the ruined structure of our previous existence.

8 **Purple eyes** berries.

10 **dearer** an anachronism, used in the sense 'more seriously' as well as in the commoner sense 'more valuable'.

12 **distills** drops, lets fall (especially of honey).

13 **He** Christ.

14 **combs** honeycombs.

'My own heart'

Here the mood differs from that found in previous poems in the 'Sonnets of Desolation' sequence. There is less of an accent on describing distress, more interest in how to establish the conditions which might help the poet regain equanimity and calm. Where does he hope to rediscover such peace? It is left unspoken, but the final image of the sonnet provides a haunting glimpse of natural beauty, a sense of the **inscape** in creation (see Interpretations pp. 151–53), pointedly absent from the other poems in this sequence.

3–4 Does the tortured syntax (arrangement of words) here heighten or mock the sense of torment?

5–8 This second quatrain is compressed so the meanings can be hard to get at. You probably need to insert a word like 'world' after *comfortless* (6) and read the *world of wet* (8) as a Hopkins coinage – characteristically highlighted through alliteration – for the sea, undrinkable water.

9 **poor Jackself** Other texts use *Jack* as a dismissive term for plain, everyday human nature. (See *That Nature is a Heraclitean Fire and of the comfort of the Resurrection*, p. 63, 23 and *The Shepherd's Brow*, p. 65, 11.)

11 **root-room** the metaphor, significantly, taken from nature and organic growth; *comfort* seen as a plant that might yet *root* in the soul.

   size grow.

14 **Betweenpie** a striking coinage; Hopkins is using a verb, 'to pie', in the sense to possess variegated colouring (see *Pied Beauty*, p. 35). Adding 'between' to create the compound term probably gives the word the sense 'making things appear alternately light and dark'. Skies often have this effect on mountains when the sun's rays are intermittently blocked by cloud. We are made to work for the meaning Hopkins is creating here.

Spelt from Sibyl's Leaves

Like the night scene which, in part, it aims to describe, this sonnet can appear dark and dense. It evokes sunset and the beginnings of night; out of this develop thoughts about the implications for human consciousness. As elsewhere, the octet–sestet relationship can be seen in terms of physical evocation leading the poet's mind to spiritual, ethical reflection. The characteristic development is from inanimate nature to human existence and its links with the divine, creative powers sustaining the world.

The actual title is (intentionally?) puzzling and oblique. *Spelt*, in connection with the Sibyl and her Leaves, suggests divination: the interpretation of omens in order to foretell future events. In ancient mythology the Sibylline Leaves were the palm leaves on which prophecies about the end of the world were written in Greek. In the medieval Latin hymn about the Last Judgement, the *Dies Irae* (Day of Wrath), the Sibyl is mentioned as an authority who has foreseen the terrors of that day. Time will end and God will sit in judgement on all human beings, judging some to join him in Paradise for eternity, others to experience the everlasting torments of Hell. The sestet is heavily coloured by such powerful ideas of judgement and damnation.

Hopkins recognized the dramatic qualities of this sonnet and its subject matter. Throughout, the lines are extended, giving an impression of a much longer poem, even though it is without the additions he used to lengthen other late sonnets (see Notes to *Harry Ploughman*, p. 114). Hopkins was sensitive to the need for effective recitation too as seen in this comment to Bridges:

> above all remember what applies to all my verse, that it is, as living art should be, made for performance and that its performance is not reading with the eye but loud, leisurely, poetical (not rhetorical) recitation, with long rests, long dwells on the rhyme and other marked syllables... This sonnet shd. be almost sung...
>
> (Letter to Robert Bridges, 11 December 1886)

1 A sense of drama from the start: the opening line is a sequence of multi-syllabled adjectives, and nothing else, employed to qualify *Evening* at the start of the second line, a tantalizing build-up.

Earnest high, lofty.

attuneable able to be harmonized, a Hopkins coinage.

stupendous literally, causing terror and amazement.

3 **hornlight... hoarlight** yellow glow from a lantern; greyish-white glow as from hoarfrost.

4 **Waste** fade.

earlstars major stars of the visible constellations.

5 **dapple** the mix and mingling of things – lights, textures, colours (see *dappled things* in *Pied Beauty*, p. 35, 1).

6 **throughther** contraction for 'throughout her', i.e. the earth?

self individual self-consciousness, as elsewhere, a central issue.

7 **Disremembering** forgetting, another dialect term.

9 **dragonish** Dragons symbolize the dark forces evoked in Revelation as the final conflict between good and evil occurs at the end of time.

damask a verb, literally to put ornate (Arabic) patterns on a sword-blade.

10 **our oracle!** In Virgil's Latin epic poem the *Aeneid* the hero,

Aeneas, is led into the underworld by the Sibyl of Cumae to
see his dead father.

11 **part, pen, pack** The basic idea is the sorting of the sheep
from the goats (see Matthew 25), the elect going to Heaven, the
damned going to Hell at the Last Judgement (so *flocks... folds*
12).

13 **ware** aware of or beware!

14 **selfwrung, selfstrung** dramatic images of Hell as Hopkins
conceived it. His own depressions led him to reflect with
personal engagement on the idea that the ultimate torture was
the fact of permanent estrangement from God's love. Hell, the
place of punishment, becomes the eternally isolated and lonely
self, tortured by its own unending thoughts of loss and regret
(see '*My own heart*', p. 59, 3–4 for a similar perception, there
applied explicitly to Hopkins's own situation).

Harry Ploughman

Like *Tom's Garland*, the next poem in this selection, and the
sonnet *That Nature is a Heraclitean Fire and of the comfort of the
Resurrection*, Hopkins expands the sonnet form considerably here
by a series of codas. The result: a sonnet some way over fourteen
lines long, which still retains the statement-development
relationship between its elements which characterizes most of
Hopkins's sonnets. As with more conventional sonnets, only
four rhymes are used throughout. This use of codas marks the
opposite process from the condensing approach employed earlier
in the 'curtal' sonnets *Pied Beauty* and *Peace*.

In a letter, Hopkins said that he had written *a direct picture of
a ploughman, without afterthought*. After stressing that it was
composed *for recital and not for perusal* (see his comments on
performance, in the Notes to *Spelt from Sibyl's Leaves*, pp. 112–13),
he commented that *perhaps it will strike you as intolerably violent
and artificial*. Does this suggestion of violence, artificiality, echo
any of your own reactions to this sonnet? Have you found any
more to the poem than highly involved description?

1 **hurdle**   willow twigs twisted into portable fencing.
   broth   a strange word here?
   Flue   is an old term for down, so here, probably, 'hair'.
2 **rack of ribs**   ribcage.
3 **Rope-over thigh**   visual image of rope-like thigh muscles?
   knee-nave   kneecap (an old sense of 'nave' is the hub of a
   wheel).
7 **onewhere**   in one place; in another place.
   curded   becoming knotted, bunched, muscles vividly
   compared to milk becoming like curd.
9 **beechbole**   trunk of a beech tree, often used for ships' masts
   because of their combination of strength and straightness,
   qualities here applied to the ploughman.
   rollcall   Like *crew* (5) this suggests the various limbs and
   muscle groups as the component members of a military unit,
   working effectively only when under the command of a single
   leader. St Paul's image of believers as the constituent parts of
   the body of Christ (Romans 12:4–5) may also be relevant here.
14 **crossbridle**   tangle (of the plough's reins).
15 **lilylocks**   blond hair.
16 **Churlsgrace**   the natural grace of the peasant; it might be
   helpful to look again at Hopkins's reflections on physical grace
   in the sonnet *To what serves Mortal Beauty?* (p. 56).
   it   i.e. the *churlsgrace*; controlling his feet as they race over the
   earth behind the plough (*cragiron* 18).
   Amansstrength   What might be Hopkins's reasons for
   contracting three words into one here?

Tom's Garland

Here Hopkins sustains a level of complexity in both thought and
technique that led his early admirers to expressions of
bafflement. As with the previous poem, codas are used to extend
the physical range of the sonnet, now twenty lines, while the
verbal technique becomes progressively more cryptic and
condensed. Whether the style points to the direction Hopkins's
poetry would have taken had he lived longer it is impossible to

say; it may be significant that in his very last poem, *To R. B.* (p. 65), he reverts to a more accessible, even traditional approach to the sonnet.

The puzzlement of his contemporaries has had one helpful outcome for later readers, however, in that it provoked Hopkins into 'unpacking' the ideas within the sonnet in his correspondence. Before setting out his own paraphrase of the sonnet, Hopkins expressed regret about the lack of comprehension in his two readers, Robert Bridges and the Anglican priest R. W. Dixon:

> It is plain I must go no further on this road: if you and he cannot understand me, who will? Yet, declaimed, the strange constructions would be dramatic and effective.
>
> **(Letter to Robert Bridges, 10 February 1888)**

Notice the stress here on *declaimed*; like the comments Hopkins made about performance in connection with *Spelt from Sibyl's Leaves* and *Harry Ploughman* (see Notes, p. 112 and p. 114), it clearly underlines the importance he attached to the aural dimension in poetry, its 'musicality', the sensuous dimension of verse spoken aloud and heard (see also Interpretations pp. 145–6).

It is probably best to regard what Hopkins goes on to say in this letter as 'scaffolding' to help with your own reading of this poem. His comments certainly do not – and were never meant to – exhaust all the possible meanings which readers can discover in the poem. They simply offer an orientation as to Hopkins's preoccupations:

> ... the commonwealth or well-ordered human society is like one man; a body with many members and each its function; some higher, some lower, but all honourable, from the honour which belongs to the whole. The head is the sovereign... we must then imagine this head as bare... and covered... only with the sun and stars, of which the crown is a symbol; it has an enormous hat or skull cap, the vault of heaven. The foot is the daylabourer... armed with hobnail boots, because it has to wear

and be worn by the ground; which again is symbolical; for it is navvies or daylabourers who... mainly trench, tunnel, blast, and in other ways disfigure, 'mammock' the earth and... stamp it with their footprints... Therefore the scene of the poem is laid at evening, when they are giving over work and one after another pile their picks... knocking sparks out of mother earth not now by labour... but by the mere footing... Here... the action of the mind mimics that of the labourer – surveys his lot, low but free from care; then by a sudden strong act throws it over the shoulder...

(Letter to Robert Bridges, 10 February 1888)

1 **garlanded** *And the garlands of nails they wear are therefore the visible badge of the place they fill, the lowest in the commonwealth*... i.e. the studded sole of Tom's workboot.

2 **fallowbootfellow** a contraction/invention for a workmate (*bootfellow*) whose labour is for the time being over (*fallow*).

3 **rockfire** sparks.

9 **lacklevel** absence of equality, equal shares in goods or wealth.

12 **no way sped** no way assisted, helped.

15 **Undenizened** outcast, homeless.

19–20 The thought in this final couplet has an explicit social and political message behind it, best expressed by Hopkins in his letter:

But presently I remember that this is all very well for those who are in, however low in, the Commonwealth and share in any way in the common weal; but that the curse of our times is that many do not share it, that they are outcasts from it and have neither security nor splendour; that they share care with the high and obscurity with the low, but wealth or comfort with neither. And this state of things, I say, is the origin of Loafers, Tramps, Cornerboys, Roughs, Socialists and other pests of society.

(Letter to Robert Bridges, 10 February 1888)

Those alienated from society through unemployment either despair and grow apathetic (*Hangdog dull*) or, worse, become angrily disaffected, revolutionaries and malcontents (*Manwolf*).

Hopkins has no remedies, but from direct personal experience – not least from his time in a poor Liverpool parish – he recognizes the malignant repercussions of unemployment. Much earlier than this, in August 1871, he commented in a letter to Robert Bridges that he felt the aims, if not the means, of communism were just:

> ... it is a dreadful thing for the greatest and most necessary part of a very rich nation to live a hard life without dignity, knowledge, comforts, delight, or hopes in the midst of plenty – which plenty they make. They profess that they do not care what they wreck and burn, the old civilization and order must be destroyed. This is a dreadful look out but what has the old civilization done for them?

That Nature is a Heraclitean Fire and of the comfort of the Resurrection

An arresting title for an arresting poem. Alongside *Tom's Garland* and *Harry Ploughman*, this poem represents the most ambitious of Hopkins's experiments with the sonnet as a poetic form. Like those other poems, it confronts its readers with a variety of challenges and potential pleasures: technique pushed further than ever, dizzy exuberance in the language and imagery, and densely original lines of thought.

Two basic pulses emerge: Hopkins's sense of the transience and diversity of natural phenomena, dazzlingly captured in the opening nine lines; and his conviction that in a universe prolific with such finite, unstable phenomena, belief in Christ's resurrection alone offers the soul of man the chance of an eternal, stable existence. You might interpret all of this as the anguish and doubt of the 'Sonnets of Desolation' seemingly transcended and conquered by the bubbling energy of a sonnet confidently linking an early Greek scientific thinker and the essential Christian doctrine of redemption. But it might just be a desperate attempt to regain equilibrium, after the suicidal depths of those poems, through verbal and intellectual gymnastics. Which seems the more plausible reading?

1 **chevy** scamper, chase.

3 **roughcast** lime and gravel for coating walls, often painted over with whitewash.

4 **Shivelights** splinters of light.
shadowtackle another invention; patterns of shadow?

6–7 A precisely organized description of the process by which mud eventually reverts to dust.

8 **Squadroned** from armies of boots?

9 **Footfretted** invention again; patterns in earth made by passing feet.
Million-fueled Heraclitus' ideas are known only through a few surviving fragments; in one of them he refers to the earth as a huge bonfire (fragment 220).

10 **clearest-selved** *self* and *selve* are important terms for Hopkins; mankind is here seen as the most individualized, personally distinctive, item in the created universe (look again at the sonnet 'As kingfishers catch fire', p. 32 especially line 7).

13–14 **that shone/Sheer off, disseveral** again, each human personality a brilliant star, each quite distinct (*disseveral*).

15 **stark** strong, firm.

18 You have only to think back to the contexts of Hopkins's two most ambitious poems to appreciate his horror of shipwreck and drowning. Here the metaphor is of a man's life as a ship in danger, the promise held out by Christ's resurrection a lighthouse signal, A *beacon, an eternal beam* (19), the one chance of eventual safety.

20 **residuary** remaining; overtones of death and decay increased by the word's associations with wills or legacies.

22 The central Christian doctrine which erupts so often into Hopkins's poetry; the incarnation, God becoming a human in the person of Christ, as the central fact of all history, the fact that makes possible an eternal existence with God for the human soul.

23 **This Jack, joke, poor potsherd, patch** the chiming effect of 'Cynghannedd' is conspicuous here (see Interpretations p. 144). As elsewhere *Jack* (see Note to line 9 of 'My own heart', p. 111)

used as a shorthand for the typical, fallen human being, a kind of 'everyman'; *potsherd* is a broken piece or shard of earthenware, used in Job as an image of humanity as a flawed aspect of creation. The sharpness is enhanced by alliteration and the chiming effect of *Jack, joke* (Hopkins is dismissive of himself here) while *patch* is an old term for a fool, a twit.

23–4 **immortal diamond** The contrast is dramatic; from *mortal trash* (19), *joke... patch... matchwood* (23) to the idea of something precious, brilliant, enduring for eternity. One of Hopkins's most powerful conclusions, or an over-dramatized ending, too reliant on violent extremes in the imagery?

Justus quidem tu es, Domine,

The Latin epigraph that forms the title partially translated in line 1, is from the Old Testament prophet, Jeremiah 12:1, where God is taken to task for his apparent lack of justice or fair play. *You are indeed just lord if I argue with you; yet argue I must; why do the affairs of the wicked prosper...?* The directness with which Hopkins addresses God here, variously imploring, reproaching and querying, results in a text of uncharacteristic explicitness. You might even want to think about it in dramatic terms, as a monologue.

Writing to Robert Bridges in March 1889 soon after completing the poem, Hopkins commented that *it must be read* adagio molto (very slowly) *and with great stress*. Bridges was later to speak of the sonnet as *an address to God, most powerful and plaintive*. Only in *The Wreck of the Deutschland* does Hopkins set out as here by directly addressing God; there is a much less provocative, dramatic invocation at the start of *The Loss of the Eurydice* (see Notes to both poems, p. 67 and p. 89). The vocabulary employed to address God is also significant: *Lord* (1), *sir* (2), *thou my friend* (5), *thou lord of life* (14). What part do these very different terms play in the moods of the sonnet? And what might the whole poem suggest about Hopkins's state of mind during the spring of his last year?

The questioning of divine justice we read in Jeremiah and again at the start of the sonnet is called 'theodicy'. On what grounds does Hopkins seem to be questioning that justice here?

4 **Disappointment**   the key 'tonal' word of the poem? See comments on line 13.
7 **sots and thralls**   (drunken) fools and slaves.
9 **brakes**   thickets.
11 **fretty chervil**   cow parsley with serrated leaves.
13 **Time's eunuch**   Matthew 19:12 speaks of those who *become as eunuchs for the kingdom of God*. Hopkins uses the term meaning an emasculated, so sterile, servant, to evoke his sense of his condition. To be *Time's eunuch* involves the idea of being an unproductive slave of mortality itself, conscious of life passing with goals unrealized. The phrase conveys a sense of futility, even maybe of self-contempt. Writing to Bridges in January 1888, Hopkins refers to himself as a *eunuch – but it is for the kingdom of heaven's sake*. In the same letter he declares *all impulse fails me: I can give myself no sufficient reason for going on. Nothing comes...* An earlier letter to Bridges, from September 1885, includes the graphic and candid revelation... *it kills me to be time's eunuch and never to beget*. Most powerfully of all, just three months prior to writing this sonnet, Hopkins disclosed in notes written on New Year's Day 1889 a desolating sense of personal failure:

What is my wretched life? Five wasted years have passed almost in Ireland. I am ashamed of the little I have done... All my undertakings miscarry: I am like a straining eunuch. I wish then for death: yet if I died now I should die imperfect, no master of myself, and that is the worst failure of all. O my God, look down on me.

from *Sermons and Devotional Writings*

'The shepherd's brow'

Written in the final months of his life, like the sonnets *Justus quidem tu es, Domine* and *To R. B.*, Hopkins seems preoccupied here with expressing a mood of disaffection with mankind: at fallen, corrupt human nature, and especially at himself as one embodiment of it. The mood is bleak and unforgiving; the joyful vision of creation which animates so many of the previous poems in this selection has, temporarily or otherwise, been replaced by a dark and cynical view of the world. The disparaging, self-deprecatory tone is particularly well caught in the final couplet.

Robert Bridges, Hopkins's first editor, did not take to this poem at all. He set it aside in his edition of 1918 with the unfinished poems and fragments, arguing that *...this must have been thrown off one day in a cynical mood, which he would not have wished to intrude among his last serious poems.* This might form a good starting point for discussion: how far as a reader would you want to argue for or against Bridges's judgement?

1 **fronting** confronting, facing up to.
   owns not possesses, more likely acknowledges, admits (like own up).
3 **Angels** the fall of the rebellious angels from Heaven.
5 **scaffold** in the senses of 'framework' and 'place of execution'; look again at the opening of *The Caged Skylark* (p. 35).
7 *memento mori* literally, a reminder of one's death.
8 **bass** lowest part in a harmony, but also 'base' as in vile, low?
   viol medieval stringed instrument, precursor of violin, cello etc. In some translations of the Old Testament, the word is used to describe a harp or lyre which accompanied mourning or lamentation.
11 **Jack** Look again at the use of this term in the sonnets *'My own heart'* (p. 59) and *That Nature is a Heraclitean Fire and of the comfort of the Resurrection* (p. 63); in each instance, a kind of shorthand for sinful human nature.

mate   implying relationships between men and women
reduced to their most basic, reproductive terms?
hussy   derived from 'housewife', and presumably meant by
Hopkins as a female counterpart to *Jack*.

13 **masque**   dramatic and musical entertainment; with the
implication that human existence is a meaningless show, a
worthless fiction.

To R. B.

This is Hopkins's last poem, written in April 1889, just seven
weeks before his final illness and death. Again, note the return to
a traditional sonnet formula in terms of its length, and the syntax
and rhythms employed. R. B. is Robert Bridges, whom Hopkins
first met as an undergraduate at Oxford (they were both born in
1844) and with whom Hopkins corresponded from 1865 until his
death. The mood here contrasts tellingly with that of the
previous poem, despite the fact that both were written about the
same time – something which may well have influenced Bridges
in his attitude to the status of that poem in his 1918 edition
(see p. 122).

   This is a special poem in Hopkins's output, and not just
because it is his last. It is the one surviving poem in which he
celebrates his own creativity, however fitful, as a writer, the
ecstasy of inspiration and its painful infrequency. Whereas the
sonnet *Justus quidem tu es, Domine,* from the same year, laments
spiritual and creative drought, here the tone adopted is gentler,
more resigned. After the dramatic spiritual and emotional
landscapes drawn in many of his other later sonnets, Hopkins
offers his friend and supporter a sense of his own hard-won
equanimity, his acceptance of creative genius as a two-edged gift
from God. It would be futile to speculate about the extent to
which Hopkins knew he had little time left to live, but it is hard
to read this sonnet without experiencing a strong sense of
valediction, of leave-taking. Bridges was himself later to

comment in a letter that even if the tone of the sonnet did not explicitly suggest *foreboding*, it was still *full of a strange fitness for the end*.

1–4 The metaphor developed is of the poem as the child of a momentary union between inspiration and the writer's mind; once the seed from the former has fertilized the egg from the latter, a long period of gestation occurs before the actual 'birth'.

6 **combs** grooms, prepares; commentators have discussed at length just how a mother can *comb* her as yet unborn child. Bridges suggested the revision 'moulds'. Which seems better to you?

7 **widow** continuing the opening metaphor, the mind now seen as the widow of the momentary inspiration, *The fine delight that fathers thought* of line 1.

9 **muse** poetry.

10 **want** both 'desire' and 'lack'.

12 **the roll, the rise, the carol** terms from ornithology, describing display and mating rituals in the spring. Note the swelling rhythmical effect of lengthening syllables in the line.

13 **My winter world** Hopkins's own inert and sterile condition as a writer.

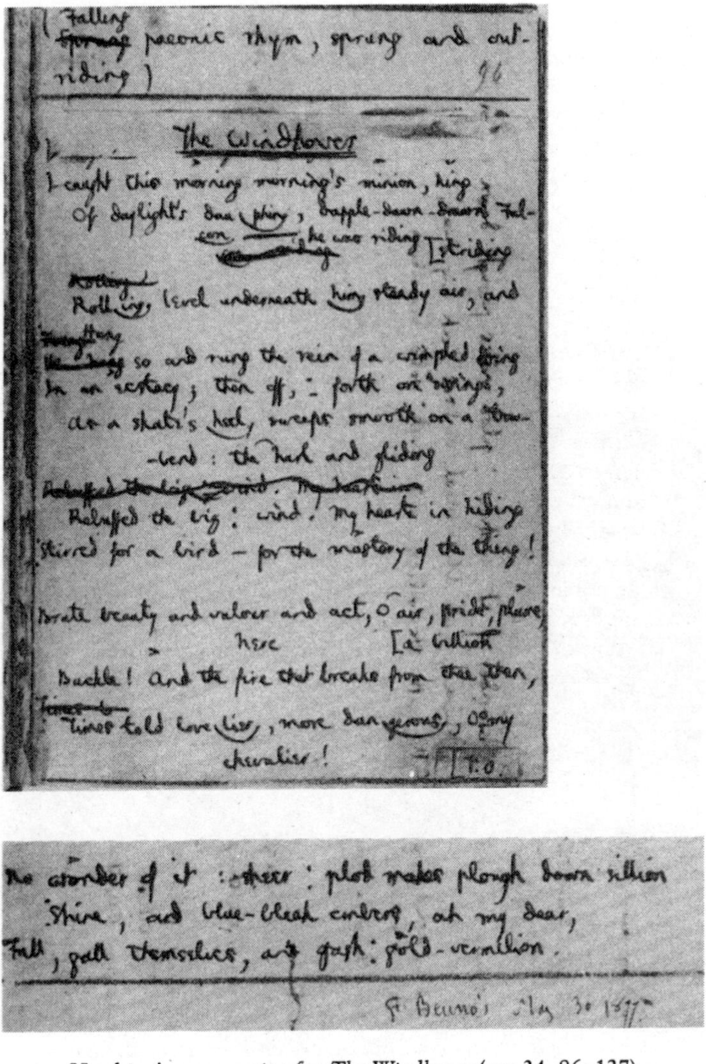
(Falling paeonic rhythm, sprung and outriding)

The Windhover

I caught this morning morning's minion, king-
Of daylight's dauphin, dapple-dawn-drawn Falcon, he was riding [striding
Rolling level underneath him steady air, and
so and rung the rein of a wimpled wing
In an ecstasy; then off, forth on swing,
As a skate's heel, sweeps smooth on a bow-bend: the hurl and gliding
Rebuffed the big wind. My heart in hiding
Stirred for a bird — for the mastery of the thing!

Brute beauty and valour and act, O air, pride, plume, here
Buckle! And the fire that breaks from thee then, [a billion
Times told lovelier, more dangerous, O my chevalier!

T.O.

No wonder of it: sheer plod makes plough down sillion
Shine, and blue-bleak embers, ah my dear,
Fall, gall themselves, and gash gold-vermilion.

St Beuno's May 30 1877

Hopkins's manuscript for *The Windhover* (pp. 34, 86, 127)

Away in the lovable west (*The Wreck of the Deutschland* line 185): this part of Clwyd around St Beuno's College provided the aesthetic inspiration behind such poems as *The Windhover* (p. 34).

Interpretations

This part of the book aims to provide you with some guidance as you reflect on Hopkins's poetry and try to make sense of it for yourself. It should help you develop an informed sense of the technical skills displayed in the poems – Hopkins's distinctive style with language, sound and rhythm – as well as an understanding of the central concepts and insights that largely define his preoccupations as a poet. This section also aims to give you a sense of the wide range of meanings different readers have found – and continue to find – in his poems.

Reading Hopkins – *The Windhover*

This initial section has two specific aims. The first is to encourage you to start thinking critically about a poem that Hopkins considered among his finest, and that subsequent criticism has also regarded as particularly significant in his output. The second is to look at the idea of 'interpretation' – the process by which readers come to develop their readings of a literary text – by exploring in detail the accounts given of the poem by three very different readers.

First then, the focus is on ways of approaching and engaging with this text. This opening section assumes you have read *The Windhover*. You might find it helpful to have the poem in front of you as you look at this section.

That meaning relies on context is illustrated by the opening. Because the title refers to a bird of prey, the words *I caught this morning* (1) imply snaring – an ironic association given the subject of the description, a hunting bird. Only from the end of the second line on do we find that the event described is the distinctive flight behaviour of the kestrel. The poet has *caught* (1) the bird only in the sense of glimpsing it unexpectedly for an instant.

Activity

Look at the opening two lines of the poem. To what extent does Hopkins try to grab your attention on reading this text?

Discussion

Some possible starting points might well include:

1   Drama: the poem is immediately personal; it is about someone, the *I* (1) who starts things off. You read of a recent personal experience. Maybe simple curiosity urges you on?
2   Rhythm: fast, urgent? Try reading these lines at a slow pace; it is very difficult! The impetus is headlong; motion is irresistible.
3   Rhyming: the *-ing* sound is conspicuous. Assume it is deliberate; even if you cannot find a reason for the repetition, at the very least the technique sharpens your attention in reading.
4   Vocabulary: simple and sophisticated. If *minion* (1) and *dauphin* (2) are unfamiliar, look them up then think about a possible link with the word *kingdom* (1–2) which straddles these lines.
5   Sound: look again at the phrase *dapple-dawn-drawn Falcon* (2), alliteration with internal rhythm. The effect is both emphatic and deliberate.

The lines describing the motions of the kestrel suggest a mood verging on intoxication, an observer transfixed by the beauty of the bird's easy movement, keen to capture both that movement and the intense feelings it stirs through the language and rhythms used. The pride identified in the kestrel leads Hopkins to portray him on horseback, a commanding figure ushering in the brilliance of sunlight (*riding... striding... rung upon the rein* [2–4]). But more than this, the bird's facility indirectly suggests the way the poet regards himself: *My heart in hiding/Stirred for a bird, – the achieve of, the mastery of the thing!* (7–8). An envious longing in the poet-observer? What if the kestrel's flight represents to the poet everything he is not? In that case, this celebration of 'completeness' might be a more complex matter. Something more has happened to the poet than sighting a kestrel's flight: something urgent, especially memorable.

Activity

List some of the reasons why Hopkins seems so attracted to the kestrel. Then think about whether the dedication to *Christ our Lord* makes any difference to the way you read the poem.

Discussion

Reasons for this attraction might include some or all of the following:
1   Aerial virtuosity; ease and authority of motion.
2   Show of power and facility in an environment where the poet has none.
3   Link with start of day; new beginnings and new life, perhaps tied in with bird's energy and grace.
4   Sheer physical beauty of the creature.

What does the dedication add to all of this? It establishes a religious context. We know that the poet is a Christian, with beliefs about the divine informing physical nature yet distinct from it. The final six lines offer the acid test; if you disregard the dedication and anything you may know of the author's life, what interpretation makes most sense of these lines to you: one incorporating some reference to a Christian scheme of values or one which takes the words and images purely at face value? (There is further discussion around this point in the Readings section below.)

Transfixed by the beautiful in nature, embodied in the kestrel, the poet-observer is even more stirred by awareness of the supernatural force through which the kestrel's powerful beauty is sustained. A useful term might be 'epiphany': a revelation of the divine amid the everyday realities of transient nature. So if the opening section, the octet of the sonnet, evokes the 'natural' context, and the first half of this final part (the final six lines – the sestet) suggests elements of 'supernatural' experience within that context, as in an epiphany, what about the final lines?

Is something like an epiphany suggested in lines 13–14? Is the metaphor of lifeless embers from a fire (note the fusion of sound and sense in the alliteration of *blue-bleak* [13]), splitting apart to disclose heat within, a symbol for what an epiphany might be like? Hopkins's meaning remains complex. Colourless, 'dead' embers can break to show heat; but *Fall, gall themselves, and gash gold-vermilion* (14)? Dramatic terms for describing so ordinary a phenomenon as this?

Unless, out of the ordinary can break the extraordinary, from the natural a glimpse of the supernatural. *Vermilion* (14) – blood? Remember the dedication: within the beliefs so important to Hopkins was the claim that Christ, the Son of God, sacrificed himself to repair the relationship between mankind and God, nature and supernature. What of the *sheer plod* (12)? As a priest, Hopkins's life was grounded in obedience, submission to authority; perhaps the metaphor of the humdrum plough, given a special sheen through the action of breaking the soil, mirrors his sense of his own outwardly humdrum, routine-driven life?

What have we discovered? A deep awareness of nature, enhanced by a poet aware of his own limits and the unlimited power of God: it seems reasonable to argue that the epiphany from which the sonnet springs reminds the poet not just of the divine creativity sustaining nature; he is also reminded of his own limitations. Envy at the kestrel's prowess is contained within the believer's sense of the divine; faith insists that his relationship *to Christ our Lord* will save him from the inadequacies he recognizes in himself, inadequacies which the kestrel's flight might only have intensified.

You can see from what has been outlined in this introduction that the poem poses many questions: if you are reading it carefully, responding to the complex pattern of words, images and strong rhythms, it is inevitable that you will find yourself asking questions about particular aspects – the micro-organization of the sonnet – as well as about its overall shape and purpose. It is inevitable that a careful reading, or a succession of such readings, will provoke puzzlement as much as insights or understanding.

Since the poem was first published in 1918, it has met the test of all great literature – been read, discussed, analysed and argued over by generations of new readers. In reading *The Windhover* and reaching your own understanding of its meaning you have interpreted it; and in interpreting the poem you have joined a community of readers and critics over the years who have asked all sorts of questions of the poem and reached all sorts of answers.

The purpose of the next section of the introduction is to present you with a small sample of the different readings of the poem that have been published and so have contributed to ongoing debate both about the meaning of this single poem and more widely about the particular qualities to be found in Hopkins's poetic output.

Reading *The Windhover*: three accounts

One early reader (his thinking on the poem was first published in 1926) who valued what he regarded as the 'experimental' quality in Hopkins's poems, wrote:

> The dedication [To Christ our Lord] at first sight is puzzling. Hopkins said of this poem that it was the best thing he ever wrote, which is to me in part the explanation. It sounds like an echo of the offering made eleven years ago when his early poems were burnt. For a while I thought that the apostrophe, *O my chevalier...* had reference to Christ. I now take it to refer only to the poet, though the moral ideal, embodied of course for Hopkins in Christ, is before the mind.

In this interpretation two particular elements have been highlighted as 'keys' to the underlying meaning – the dedication (which this reader sees as suggesting a sacrifice of some kind on

Hopkins's part) and the phrase O *my chevalier* – understood as referring not to Christ or the kestrel, but to the poet himself. His account also finds particular significance in another phrase towards the close of the octet:

> *My heart in hiding...* Why in hiding? Hiding from what? Does this link up with *a billion times told lovelier, more dangerous, O my chevalier!*? What is the greater danger and what the less? I should say that the poet's heart is in hiding from Life, has chosen a safer way, and that the greater danger is the greater exposure to temptation and error that a more adventurous, less sheltered course (sheltered by Faith?) brings with it...

So the interpretation emerging here presents an account of the poem where the central theme (or possibly preoccupation) seems to be the poet's ambivalent attitude to his priestly vocation. It is an ambivalence somehow provoked by the sight of the kestrel in flight – totally free, in his element, at one with nature, fulfilling his true purpose – everything that (in this reading) the poet is not. Additional evidence for this account is found in the final three lines, which 'carry the thought of the achievement possible through renunciation further': the 'image of the ash-covered fire' (i.e. Hopkins's *blue-bleak embers*) is seen as showing 'why the dangers of the inner life are greater'. This is how the account concludes:

> The close has a strange, weary, almost exhausted rhythm, and the word *gall* has an extraordinary force, bringing out painfully the shock with which the sight of the soaring bird has jarred the poet into an unappeased discontent.

For this reader, then, the real concern of the poet is not with the kestrel, not even with Christ (despite the focus given to the dedication), but with his sense of himself – and the overall direction of the reading is summed up in that final phrase, 'unappeased discontent'. In this reading the poem is as much a dirge, or elegy, lamenting the poet's frustration and inadequacy as it is a celebration of nature. In reaching this conclusion the reader has gone well beyond the immediate evidence of the text into speculation about Hopkins's mental or emotional state, based at least in part on the notion (prejudice?) that the poet's religious beliefs are in direct conflict with his impulses as a poet. Indeed, a little later in this account, considering Hopkins's work more widely, this reader articulates the view 'that the poet in him was often oppressed and stifled by the priest'. This leads him to the unequivocal conclusion 'In this sense all Hopkins's poems are poems of defeat'.

Activity

How might you go about evaluating the reading of *The Windhover* outlined above?

Discussion

The reading has the merit of being succinct and clearly expressed – in that respect, a model for any student! However, it is hard to accept the argument developed unless you take as a premise – something understood to be the case – the idea that Hopkins's personality was torn between the contrary impulses of poetry and religion. The former entailed the suppression or denial of the latter. If you accept this rather simplistic account, with its 'biographical' reference to Hopkins's earlier decision (as disclosed in a letter) to destroy manuscripts of poems when he became a priest, then the overall logic of this reading makes sense. *The Windhover* emerges as a very special kind of poem, in which the inner spiritual conflict is temporarily resolved, or suspended, through a set of images whose interaction depicts and illuminates the conflict. But the cost of accepting such a reading is to identify Hopkins as 'a poet of defeat' – and this is, perhaps, too high a price to pay. There is a simple enough test: look at the other poems in this selection, and ask yourself whether the concept of 'defeat' – with so much meaning invested in the single phrase *my heart in hiding* – helps you gain a more comprehensive or complete understanding of Hopkins's work.

A second relatively early, but even more influential, account of *The Windhover* was written by a student of the first reader, and published in 1930. Like the critic whose interpretation you have just studied, this second account of the poem is written from a perspective that is antagonistic to Hopkins's beliefs. The principal difference between the two readings centres on the second reader's acute interest in the concept of **ambiguity** as one of the defining features of great poetry. He sees in *The Windhover* a striking instance of one particular form of ambiguity, where the two senses of a word used by a poet are in effect opposite to each other, and so are exploited to reveal the contrary, divided nature of the poet's own mind.

The key ambiguous term focused on in this analysis of the poem is *Buckle* near the start of the sestet:

> *Buckle* admits of two tenses and two meanings: 'they do buckle here', or, 'come, and buckle yourself here', *buckle* like a military belt for the discipline of heroic activity, and *buckle* like a bicycle wheel, 'make useless, distorted and incapable of its natural motion'. *Here* may mean 'in the case of the bird', or 'in the case of the Jesuit'; then 'when you have become like the bird', or 'when you have become like the Jesuit'. *Chevalier* personifies either physical or spiritual activity; Christ riding to Jerusalem, or the cavalryman ready for the charge; Pegasus, or the Windhover.

And when this second reader turns to the latter half of the sestet, the interpretation put on particular words and phrases again emphasizes instability, stress and suffering:

> The metaphor of the *fire* covered by ash seems most to insist on the beauty the *fire* gains when the ash falls in, when its precarious order is again shattered... The *gold* that painters have used for the haloes of saints is forced by alliteration to agree with the *gash* and the *gall* of their self-tortures; from this precarious triumph we fall again, with *vermilion*, to bleeding.

Activity

For the second reader the ambiguities he discovers in the poem are bound up with Hopkins's need 'to convey an indecision'. How well do you think this account captures the whole poem?

Discussion

We can say first and foremost that this is by any reckoning a 'brilliant' reading – alive to every nuance, clever and self-assured. But you may also find yourself asking a question or two. Like – what about the octet? If ambiguity is so vital to the inner form of this poem, why is this feature, apparently, absent from the first eight lines? And for such a sophisticated reading, isn't the account provided of the final line almost comic in its literalness? Because this reader is so determined to see an element of suffering self-sacrifice in the sestet (sharing this perspective on the poem with the first reader), the term *gash* can only admit of a single meaning (ironic in a reading of the text where ambiguity is rife!) – a slashing cut – so *vermilion* can only signify blood, and *gold* by an even odder association of ideas comes to represent a halo in an icon or religious painting. Might this be a case of a reader overlaying an already complex text with pre-conceptions hostile to the beliefs assumed to lie behind the text itself?

A third and later reader takes a very different view of *The Windhover*. Written thirty years after the two 'early' accounts you have just studied, her account of the text is informed by what they and many other readers since them had said and written about the poem and its meaning. This is an important point to note: in interpreting a text, developing and sharing your own reading of it, you are contributing to a tradition, implicitly joining a community of other readers who meet on common ground when they engage with any text – however much their separate readings may disagree.

The third reader writes as if she has decided that the poem has been the victim of too much 'interpretation'. You may just agree with her, having reflected on some of the meanings ascribed to the poem even in the two accounts you have been studying. She says she 'is disposed to be dogmatic', insisting that there is only one 'meaning' that can emerge from the poem if all its component parts are to make sense. Like our two previous readers, she identifies the word *buckle* in the first half of the sestet as pivotal to the poem's meaning – but she ascribes a very different sense to it, linking the 'new' meaning to the significance of the *AND* immediately following:

Something buckles and something breaks through. Readers who buckle belts reflect the second half of this statement, though Hopkins capitalized the *AND* between the parts... Deck or bulkheads of a ship buckle before fire breaks through; walls of a building buckle before they crash or burn. In *The Windhover* the whole material world buckles *AND the fire* – of the spiritual world – or Christ – *breaks* through. *Buckle* and *breaks* control the sestet as it subsides from the climax of spiritual illumination to the everyday imagery of the conclusion.

She proceeds to relate Hopkins's technique and purpose in *The Windhover* to his approach in the contemporary sonnets (particularly *Spring* and *The Starlight Night*) where a similar progression occurs – from rapt evocation of some feature perceived in physical nature in the octet, to reflection on its spiritual meaning in the sestet. What she clearly doesn't discover in the poem is the inner conflict over 'the Belief problem' that our earlier readers seized on as the interpretative key to the poem's essential meaning.

Her discussion explicitly sees the kestrel as an **analogue** of Christ – not, as such, a symbol. This is critical. For her the poem is *not* an allegory – at its simplest, a narrative where characters and events stand for abstractions or concepts (one familiar example – Aesop's fable of the tortoise and the hare, where the animals are allegorical representations of contrasting but recognizable human characteristics set in a narrative where the writer allows us to compare and judge them). Christ then is not depicted in the kestrel, although both the dedication and the use of the terms *minion* and *dauphin* (i.e. son rather than king/father) convey a strong analogy or parallel, where Hopkins invites his readers to imagine some kinship between the two. The subject of the octet, in other words, remains a kestrel, *falco tinnunculus*, a bird of prey, a member of the falcon family – celebrated for its aerial grace and agility – and not Christ worshipped by Hopkins as the Son of God.

By contrast for this reader, explicitly and with complete certainty, the *chevalier* Hopkins addresses in the sestet is Christ. The naturalistic frame of the octet is dramatically overtaken by an instant of epiphany, both attractive and terrifying – *lovelier, more dangerous* – as the poet momentarily experiences the supernatural breaking through the natural. She sees the poem working through two pairs of opposites: nature/supernature, or material/spiritual (octet/sestet) on the one side, exhilaration/terror on the other. Her conclusion is that

> These opposites... are not evenly balanced in the poem: the terror or pain is no more than an undertone, reflected in one epithet of Christ, in the *gall* and *gash* of the close, possibly in the predatory character as well as the daring of the hawk and in the poet's *hiding* heart. The unresolved suggestions of terror and pain give an edge to the overriding spirit of breathless admiration.

Activity

'The poem conveys one direct meaning.' Are you convinced that the interpretation outlined here offers you that single comprehensive account?

Discussion

What I find sets this reading apart is the fact that the evidence produced to validate the interpretation is drawn exclusively from the text itself. This reading does not look to details from Hopkins's life, or speculation about the problematic nature of his religious vocation, to justify itself. However, it is possible to agree with the broad outline of a reading and still find room for disagreement over the account in terms of its detailed working. It is curious, for instance, how this account neglects much of the detail in the octet – is it only there to pad out the 'naturalism' of the first part of the poem, before attention switches to the allegedly greater challenges of the sestet? Again, you might argue that she takes an overly prosaic view of the final lines – perhaps in reaction to the highly imaginative (even fanciful?) account provided by our second reader – where it seems reasonable to argue that Hopkins's colour sequence, *blue-bleak* to *gold-vermilion*, hints at something, a progression from one state to another, that is more than the dying embers disclosing heat within.

The aim of this section has been to illustrate how different readers produce different interpretations of a text by highlighting different facets, as well as by attaching a range of meanings to those facets they might agree on. Think of the key issues raised by our three readers – who is *my chevalier*? What is the best way to define or explain *buckle*? What lies behind the phrase *my heart in hiding*? What is the significance of the dedication? Yet in engaging with common questions they arrive at very different answers. And that, in essence, is what interpreting a literary text involves: using the available textual evidence to establish a reading that hopes to be both consistent – not contradicting itself – and coherent – presenting an account that makes sense.

If you are curious to discover the identities of the three readers whose accounts have been examined here, they are revealed in the Further Reading section towards the end of the book.

Different readers will continue to arrive at accounts of a poem as challenging as *The Windhover* simply because meaning isn't fixed and absolute. That, surely, is why we continue to read and study poems – just because they provoke us to discover and refine our own meanings as we respond to them.

So, one aspect of Hopkins that you might want to test out is that of a writer whose obsession with God in nature acquires special force through boldness of rhythm, of imagery, of sound. The aim of the following sections is to help you respond to such qualities in specific contexts, making connections between the distinctive voice and the vision Hopkins articulates through it.

Hopkins's poetic technique

Reading Hopkins

One of the aims of the opening section was to get you looking in some detail at the techniques Hopkins uses in *The Windhover*, and to suggest some of the ideas that stimulated him to write. The assumption was that *The Windhover* could in some senses be seen as a characteristic Hopkins poem, a poem whose technique, structure, tone and themes could also be seen working more widely in his output as a writer.

That opening discussion has highlighted three focal points:

1 the style of the poem, its verbal and rhythmic energy;
2 its stress on nature and religion;
3 the sense a reader can indirectly form of the *I* speaking in the poem.

First, then, a look at style.

Hopkins's style

The word 'style' when applied to a poet can mean many things. Here it is taken to mean the distinctive way in which the resources of language, in particular, sound and rhythm, are employed to convey meaning. Because Hopkins was a great experimenter in matters of rhythm and language, it is easy for readers new to him to be intimidated by discussions of technique; learned journals are full of articles on Hopkins's 'prosody', the technical term for the study of rhythm and metre, which can have the effect of making the whole topic seem academic and difficult. In its essentials, it is not; nor is it worth getting too concerned about the finer points of the innovative technique which Hopkins christened **sprung rhythm**. Like all discussion of the 'how' in a poem, thinking about Hopkins's approach to rhythm is justified only where it can be interestingly applied to the 'what', the focus, the theme, the concern. This approach to style will be adopted throughout this section.

Sprung rhythm

What is it? Why does Hopkins use it?

Activity

Look at the first two stanzas (lines 1–8) of *The Habit of Perfection* (p. 17); read them aloud. Note down any thoughts you have about the rhythm you find there. Then look at the octet (lines 1–8) of the sonnet *Hurrahing in Harvest* (p. 36). Do the same as for the first poem. Are there any differences? Compare your findings if possible with those of other readers.

Discussion

Reading *The Habit of Perfection* I detect a steady four-beat rhythm, the kind of metre associated with octosyllabic verse: poems in which each line contains exactly eight syllables. The effect seems light and undemanding, assisted by the regular abab rhyme in each stanza. This choice of rhythm and form necessarily involves compromise over the choice and placing of words; e.g. the phrase *Which only* (8), instead of 'which alone', seems imposed by the rhythmical scheme. The effect is smooth, calm, regular. By contrast, the rhythmical scheme in *Hurrahing in Harvest* seems more disjointed, with syllables in each line varying between ten and fourteen. The lines are therefore longer; punctuation is used to interrupt poetic flow (e.g. semicolons, lines 1–2; exclamations, lines 2–3); commas are used liberally, to slow down the tempo, to stress or accent (e.g. lines 5, 7). In place of a rhythm which achieves regular flow to suggest something fulfilled or satisfied, this seems like a rhythm imitating someone talking excitedly, pointing out things of importance, suggesting real involvement.

We can say that **sprung rhythm** involves writing lines of poetry in which the number of syllables used matters much less than the organization of stresses: the syllables deliberately chosen for emphasis by the voice. Regularity in regard to the syllabic length of each line, its quantity, becomes secondary; what matters is the regular sequence of stressed syllables, irrespective of the actual count of syllables per line.

There is more to the practice of **sprung rhythm** than this outline indicates; if you are interested in learning more about prosody in Hopkins, the best place to start is the Preface Hopkins wrote to the poems his friend Robert Bridges kept for him in manuscript (unprinted) form. That Preface is reprinted at the head of *The Wreck of the Deutschland* in each of the three complete editions of the poetry listed in the Further Reading section at the end of this book (p. 177). The questions which arise here are: why did he employ this technique, and what does it do for his poems?

Two earlier poems in this selection, *Heaven-Haven* and *The Habit of Perfection*, include no traces of this stress-based rhythmical understanding; the majority of the poems written from the mid-1870s onwards, starting with *The Wreck of the Deutschland*, use this technique in increasingly ambitious ways. Why does he do it? No one can say what prompted Hopkins to integrate technical conclusions he drew from reflecting on the way rhythm operated in a range of poets into the fabric of his own achievement as a poet. In a letter to R. W. Dixon (admirer and former schoolmaster) of October 1878 he commented that *I had long had haunting my ear the echo of a new rhythm which now I realized on paper*. The form that realization of a *haunting... new rhythm* took was *The Wreck of the Deutschland*. But *haunting my ear* may be a significant clue; it hardly suggests a deliberate attempt at novelty, writing in a different way just to be different. It sounds more like the unforced, unconscious originality of a creative genius, a radically new way of organizing movement in a poem which comes unbidden to the writer but which he feels compelled to accept and exploit. What do you think?

In terms of 'why?', you will for the moment have to settle for the suggestion made above that **sprung rhythm** was a liberating device for a poet working at a time when rules and conventions meant far more than they do in the more laissez-faire artistic culture of the early twenty-first century. It allowed Hopkins to introduce a dramatic 'declamatory' quality into his verse, replicating the patterns of natural human speech in a heightened or stylized manner. Discussion later shows how basic to the impact and purpose of his poems Hopkins felt the declamatory element to be: the effect of reading or hearing a poem aloud. At the same time, Hopkins retained the controlling factor of rhyme. He also held on to traditional structural devices; the majority of texts in this selection are either sonnets or longer poems organized in a formal stanza arrangement. So innovation made within well-observed boundaries; inventive radicalism over rhythm is balanced by employment of accepted poetic forms.

The sound world

It is not only in his rhythmic adventurousness that we can look at Hopkins as an original, and so think about his style as distinctive. In the sound-world created in his verse, Hopkins reveals an awareness which, like his interest in rhythm, is as much musical as literary. Discussion of *The Windhover* has suggested some of this quality; the aim here is to identify pervasive techniques and offer some ideas about why his verse might incorporate them.

Hopkins uses the techniques of alliteration and assonance, deliberately repeated consonant and vowel sounds respectively, for a variety of reasons. Sometimes it is to suggest a connection between the sound in the language and the sounds being described by the language – what you may know as onomatopoeia. Sometimes the chains of sound are there largely for emphasis, to make an aggressive undercurrent in the poem feel more aggressive, a gentle or lyrical tone seem gentler and so on. And sometimes identical sounds proliferate simply because Hopkins is a very sensuous poet; strongly believing in the musical or aural element in poetry, the texture of the sound-world he creates is vital to him, and a constitutive element in any poetic sound-world, alongside distinctive rhythms, is clearly projected repetition of particular sound patterns.

Activity

Look again at the sonnets *God's Grandeur* (p. 31) and *Pied Beauty* (p. 35). Read both aloud, several times, concentrating on the octets. Identify as many examples of alliteration and/or assonance as you can. What initial ideas do you have about why Hopkins uses these techniques here?

Discussion

Looking at the sonnet *God's Grandeur*, I can see examples of alliteration in phrases such as 'like shining from shook foil' (2); 'reck his rod' (4); 'dearest freshness deep down things' (10). There is a strong sense of assonance in 'seared with trade; bleared, smeared with toil' (6) and 'wears man's smudge and shares man's smell' (7) (both of these examples also involve alliteration). In *Pied Beauty*, an example of alliteration and assonance combined is 'couple-colour' (2). A nice example of multiple alliteration is provided by 'Landscape plotted and pieced–fold, fallow, and plough' (5). There is assonance in the echoing long vowels in 'rose-moles' (3) and in 'finches' wings' (4).

Alongside this emphasis on successive consonant/vowel patterns, intricate chains of sounds develop throughout the poem; e.g. moving, through lines 1–8, 'the chain dappled' (1), 'couple' (2), 'stipple' (3), 'plotted' (5), 'plough' (5), 'tackle' (6), 'fickle, freckled' (8), where I sense the liquid sound of the letter *l* is being deliberately exploited in a sequence of combinations, sometimes at the end of a word, sometimes at the beginning.

Sound and sense

Assuming none of these patterns is accidental or random, what is the point? Both poems involve God and nature, the former as the all-powerful creator of the latter. Nature is felt to be beautiful, worthy of veneration in its own right. Hopkins draws attention to the features he wants to highlight, stresses them for attention in reading, by building up aural connections via simple repetitions within a phrase or line, or as in the last example through elaborate sound patterning over a longer scale. The meanings become more memorable through being embodied in a highly composed framework of rhythm and sound. Scholars have linked this stress on alliteration and internal rhyme to the 'consonant chime' traditionally employed in Welsh poetry – 'Cynghanedd' (pronounced Kung-hanneth) – which Hopkins discovered during his period of study at St Beuno's College, North Wales, in the 1870s.

Links between sound and sense? Perhaps Hopkins links the features represented in the poem through common patterns of sound to suggest the idea that all things are ultimately related to each other as the work of a single creator. Assonance and alliteration, techniques for establishing 'kindredness' in word sound, might be for Hopkins useful tools for symbolizing the kindredness of all the elements making up the created world.

You may not be convinced by this line of argument; you may find it far-fetched or unnecessary. It assumes that sound patterns in a poem cannot be ends in themselves, but should be interpreted as playing a role in establishing themes; they are functional elements, contributing towards the complex of meaning represented by the poem. The hypothesis suggested here may therefore seem to you over-concerned with finding an explanation for the sound patterns in these poems; sounds do not need a rational purpose or justification, poems are not machines. End of argument.

If you adopt this view, you might want to return to the sensuous interpretation of sound in Hopkins, a view earlier highlighted in the context of a poem's musical or aural dimension. If Hopkins frequently exploits the sounds of language in his poems it is because he finds them intrinsically interesting or pleasurable. Whichever approach you adopt: sounds as sensuous ends in themselves; sounds as functional elements within an organized complex of meaning; it seems clear that sounds are at least as important to Hopkins as is the sense of the words he employs. And it may be worth noting that whereas the developing interest in **sprung rhythm** first materializes in a specific text at a specific time, *The Wreck of the Deutschland*, composed in 1875–6, the feeling for sound in his writing is strongly embedded prior to that: you need only look at a poem already discussed in terms of its rhythmic qualities, *The Habit of Perfection* (p. 17), to see this.

As in later poems, there is plentiful alliteration, assonance and chiming: the effect of echoing, subtly altering syllabic patterns, the 'Cynghanedd' mentioned on page 144. In this area, its similarity to a later poem like *Hurrahing in Harvest* is probably greater than any marked differences. There is the evidence of phrases such as *Pipe me to pastures still* (2) or *Coils, keeps, and teases simple sight* (12). The stress on similar sound-effects in *Hurrahing in Harvest* is immediately apparent: *barbarous in beauty* (1), *greeting of realer, of rounder replies* (8). What most distinguishes the two poems from each other is less sound than the context in which it is located; the **sprung rhythm** used in the later poem allows Hopkins to introduce urgencies and moments of special stress which are inevitably harder to achieve in a more regular metrical scheme. And the use of **sprung rhythm** to underline this dramatic conception of what happens in a poem is itself facilitated by the range of effects made possible through sound patterning.

Hearing versus reading

You may already have seen from the Notes to several of the poems in this selection how seriously Hopkins thought about this musical dimension of his poems. On more than one occasion he argued with sceptical admirers that the underlying sense of a text which they regarded as over-complicated or difficult could be grasped just by listening to a good reading of the poem in question. The evidence is that Hopkins differentiated between the 'heard' experience of a text and the 'read' experience. And this would give weight to the 'sensuous' argument developed earlier; Hopkins wants to project a strongly defined sound world in his poems. You might argue that the stress on sound and the innovative use of rhythm actually complement each other; the music in the poems sets out to be utterly distinctive, peculiar to its creator. It works with, but can be enjoyed separately from, the ideas which provide this music with its special themes.

Activity

The idea of a 'music' has been introduced. To develop this analysis a little more, look at the octet of the sonnet *'As kingfishers catch fire'*. There are five stresses to each line in the rhythm. Try putting these stresses into the lines, then read them, preferably several times; this is a good group activity! Note down some initial responses to links between sound and meaning in these eight lines. Then, look at the sound-commentary which follows.

Discussion

The opening line falls symmetrically into two parts, each involving multiple alliterations (*k* / *c*; *f* in the first half: *dr*, *fl* in the second). The semicolon at the end of the line emphasizes this sense of equal balance, by creating a strong endline pause, but the next line and a bit reads as a continuous phrase, with a strong alliterative effect through *r* sounds and a subtler thread picked out in the assonance chime *rim... ring* (2–3). The predominance of single-syllable words works with the five-stress rhythm to produce a clipped, brisk effect as I read it. The most notable sound feature in the remainder of line 3 is the internal rhyme *tells... bell's*, succeeded by strong alliteration on the *b* sound and another internal rhyme, this time sustained over three syllables: *hung... swung... tongue* (3–4). In addition, this sequence offers a half-rhyme echo of *ring* (3); and enforcing all of this, I have the feeling that Hopkins is establishing an onomatopoeic effect throughout lines 3–4, imitating through syllabic chimes the chiming sound of bells. By contrast, line 5 offers a break from sound decoration; it may even be that the unglamorous-sounding, prosaic *thing* used twice, may stress this switch from sensuous vocal score to something more mundane. In the following line, harder *d* sounds are softened by the liquid effect of *dwells* (6) as the endline rhyme word, while the initial stress in line 7 must be on the opening syllable, the coinage *Selves*, with the rest of the line dominated by this sibilant pattern of repeated s sounds (sibilants missing from only two words, *it* and *and*). The aural effect of the final line of the octet is determined by the repeated pronoun I (8), the sequence of strong, simple vowels – *do... me... for... that... came* (8) – and the decisive mid-line pause of the colon. Indeed, any attempt to describe the aural qualities of these lines must take account of the punctuation. Colons or semicolons are used seven times in eight lines. You can add to that count the retarding effect of the hyphen in line 7. In reading these eight lines aloud, I am aware of a great richness and range in the opening quatrain (lines 1–4), offset by a plainer texture in lines 5–8. This seems a good point at which to end an aural analysis and begin investigating the sense of the lines.

Binsey Poplars: linking sound and sense

Before leaving the issue of style, it might be worth looking at a poem other than a sonnet, where formal links between octet and sestet are irrelevant, where the closely disciplined rhyme scheme of the sonnets can be relaxed. In addition, *Binsey Poplars* might offer some pointers when thinking about the themes in the poetry.

The approach followed here is simple; one reason for reading Hopkins is that his poems often suggest vivid descriptive powers enhanced by a musical feel for sound and rhythm. How well does this text display these qualities? And, more provocatively, if such qualities do exist in the poem, is that all there is to it – a succession of pleasant sounds and rhythms?

Activity

Looking at *Binsey Poplars* (p. 42), what do you notice about sound and rhythm?

Discussion

The rhythmical range, from two to six stresses per line, gives the poem a real sense of movement, an ebb and flow variation between longer and shorter verses. Repetition and internal rhyme figure throughout, helping enforce a feeling of 'interconnectedness' in the lyric; perhaps they are also used to underline its rhythmical character (see lines 3, 5, 16). Alliteration occurs extensively throughout, itself linked to this organic quality. From the repeated *qu* and *l* sounds in lines 1–2, to the proliferation of sibilants in the closing lines, it is clear that Hopkins is keen to score a sound-picture full of links and echoes.

Overall then, movement and variety in the rhythm, patterning in the sound structure. Can we jump from these stylistic traits, now identified across a range of texts, to the actual subject matter of the poem? Discussion so far has been concerned with the idiom, the voice. But what do we hear as that voice is communicating with us?

Hopkins's themes

An entry in Hopkins's Journal for 8 April 1873 records the effect upon him of the felling of an ash tree:

> The ashtree growing in the corner of the garden was felled. It was lopped first: I heard the sound and looking out and seeing it maimed there came at that moment a great pang and I wished to die and not to see the inscapes of the world destroyed any more.

Binsey Poplars was written in response to an event that took place six years later (March 1879), but the thread of feeling connecting the two texts is obvious; by 1879 Hopkins was sufficiently accomplished a poet to channel his sense of grief and loss into an elegy, in the first instance for a line of trees by the Thames just west of Oxford, more generally though for all manifestations of natural beauty and order destroyed by human action.

Hopkins the nature poet

Every poem so far discussed has included a strong element of descriptive writing. The focus of that element each time has been Hopkins's sense of the beauty of nature. It seems right to consider Hopkins a true 'nature poet' in the sense that physical nature is never a mere backdrop in his poems, something picturesque brought in as decoration; instead, it is often at the heart of the experience Hopkins wishes to communicate.

Activity

Look at the three poems *Spring* (p. 32), *Inversnaid* (p. 47) and *Ribblesdale* (p. 50). Can you find any common threads in what the poems say about nature?

Discussion

All three poems focus on specifics; Hopkins's evocations of nature are never vague or in a wordy soft focus. In *Spring*, he peers so minutely at the birds' eggs that they *look little low heavens* (3), while the parent bird's piercing call is heard to *rinse and wring/The ear* (4–5). The highland stream observed in *Inversnaid* is visualized even to the froth formed on the surface of its pools (5–7), while the fierce motion of the stream moistens with water vapour *Wiry heathpacks, flitches of fern* (11), sensuous details caught in concise, alliterative phrasing. In *Ribblesdale*, the lush Lancashire countryside is described *with leaves throng/And louched low grass* (1–2). Throughout, there is evidence of a feeling for particulars, the significance of observed details, and of course for sound clusters which stress these details. But the poems are not simply versified descriptions of places or seasons. In *Spring*, while the first part of the sonnet does focus explicitly on the keen beauty of a time when nature is coming to life after the sterility

149

of winter, the sestet adopts a more urgent tone (see Notes p. 83) in directing attention to human beings. In *Inversnaid* three stanzas of physical description give way to a final stanza full of the same 'ecological' vision to be seen at work in *Binsey Poplars*. In *Ribblesdale*, even the octet seems more concerned with God than with nature; the following sestet is taken up with mankind as the most problematic aspect of the creation.

Nature and religion

So the continued focus on nature, grounded in such specifics as the unique flight pattern of the kestrel, the call of the lark ascending beyond sight, the shade offered by a perfect line of riverside poplars, involves a set of values as well as the writer's descriptive powers.

The religious belief informing the perception of nature has already been touched on in the initial discussion of *The Windhover* (see pp. 127–31). More generally throughout the poems in this selection, Hopkins celebrates nature as something inherently good, because created by a loving God, as inherently beautiful, its beauty also reflecting in physical forms the ideal beauty of the creator. An important conclusion follows from this. The beauty of the creation being our only sensory access to the beauty of the creator, we might be justified in seeing an element of prayer, of worship, in the way that the poems make so much of the poet's direct experience of nature. This line of argument can be used to consolidate our sense of Hopkins as a 'nature poet'. He believes that the energies and vastness of nature require an order that is willed and consciously sustained. There is an ultimate purpose; nature is not something contingent, an accidental combination of molecules, a random set of phenomena that might have been different, or might not have been at all. The universe Hopkins perceives and venerates is not that whose origins Darwin had so momentously begun analysing in *The Origin of Species* as the consequences of billions of years of random selection. In looking at Hopkins's ideas about nature, it is impossible to ignore the element of awe, respect and admiration directed towards some all-powerful creative force.

Activity

Look at the lyric *Spring and Fall* (p. 46). In the light of the previous discussion, is there anything 'religious' about the way Hopkins explores nature in the poem?

Discussion

In this poem I think Hopkins is using nature, not, as earlier mentioned, as a convenient backdrop, something pretty or decorative, but to say something about human experience. The easy but unpatronized grief of the child, experiencing natural decline and decay for the first time in the shape of autumn leaves, is symbolic of innocence. Her thoughts are *fresh* (4), her feelings spontaneous and touching. Hopkins imagines the older, more care-worn Margaret as blind to the natural sadness of autumn, yet weeping still; weeping for her own mortality and imperfection. The summing-up of the final rhyming couplet makes explicit the religious dimension at work; sin and death are the heavy realities provoking the older woman's sorrow, *It is Margaret you mourn for* (15). *Fall* is both autumn and the discovery of evil; for Hopkins this makes mankind the most problematic factor in the whole of nature.

Nature and beauty: inscape

Along with **sprung rhythm**, the other concept frequently associated with Hopkins is that of **inscape**. The word has already appeared in these Interpretations, as well as in the initial Context section. If you look back to the discussion of *Binsey Poplars* (p. 148), you will find the note from his Journal where Hopkins laments the felling of a tree, feeling he would die rather than *see the inscapes of the world destroyed any more*. The word – Hopkins coined it himself – never occurs in the poems in this selection, although it occurs frequently in the Journal and the ideas behind it influence many of the poems here. So what is **inscape**?

At its simplest, there are two linked ideas. The first is that all phenomena we can observe in nature possess some organizing secret which makes them what they are, which gives them the particular form of beauty they reveal to the observer. Prior to his coinage of the word, there are passages in the Journals where Hopkins is struggling to clarify his thinking; he worries about the organization of oak trees, desperate to find the uniquely distinctive pattern which is theirs. Then a few days later, a sense of Eureka!: *I have now found the law of the oak leaves...* (the Journal, July 1866). He finds this *law*, the key to the creator's secret in the oak tree, in the way its leaves are patterned. Hopkins has yet to find the word, but he now has the concept. **Inscape** is the underlying form, the essence, of an object; not the surface irregularities which make it one oak leaf rather than another, but the quality intrinsic to all oak leaves, what you might call their 'oak leaf-ness'. And what goes for oak leaves applies equally to kestrels, poplar trees, clouds, thrushes' eggs, ploughed fields, etc.

For Hopkins what is most real about things in the physical world is not to be found through casual observation; **inscape** is discovered through sudden, unexpected insight: the epiphany mentioned in connection with *The Windhover* on page 130. This concept of **inscape** as developed by Hopkins owes much to his preoccupation with philosophy, especially with metaphysics, the investigation of such abstract concepts as being, identity and time. As the Context section above shows, it owes much to the medieval thinker Duns Scotus and his notion of *Haecceitas*.

But the **inscape** is not obvious or self-evident, which leads on to the second key element in the concept. While anyone with eyes can see the physical detail of the object, it requires vision to experience this sense of underlying form, the essence of the object. Another Journal entry in July 1872 describes in precise detail the interior of a barn, the *big bold A's* of the timber frames, after which Hopkins makes this regretful comment: *I thought how sadly beauty of inscape was unknown and buried away from simple people and yet how near at hand it was if they had eyes to see it.*

True apprehension of beauty depends on awareness of

inscape since it is the **inscape** –the formal organizing and defining quality – which gives anything its intrinsic beauty. And linked closely to **inscape** is 'instress': the imaginative sensation experienced when an object's **inscape** is properly perceived. Only those whose vision goes beyond appearances experience the true beauty of natural phenomena; everyone else has only a glimmer, a weak reflection, of this beauty, like those who are tone-deaf or colour-blind.

Activity

Look again at the opening lines of the sonnet *God's Grandeur* (p. 31). Are there any links here with the ideas about **inscape** just discussed?

Discussion

If the account offered of **inscape** is valid, the opening three lines of this sonnet reveal Hopkins connecting the idea of the beauty experienced only when we sense the essence of something with the realization that this essence has been created by God. So a sense of natural beauty is connected directly with a religious sense of awe associated with the source of that natural beauty. But there is a problem here. If this *grandeur* (1) is seen to *flame out, like shining from shook foil* (2), is this not an image of something brilliant, vivid, unmistakable – like an electrical storm? There appears to be a contradiction: either the God-created **inscapes** are there for all to perceive and appreciate, or they are accessible only by the few with specially tuned spiritual or imaginative antennae. Which is it? Perhaps one answer to this puzzle is to say that Hopkins may not identify the beautiful exclusively with an object's **inscape**. Even surfaces may have elements of pattern or symmetry which contribute to an object's beauty. It may be that seeing even these lesser, surface patterns will lead people to connect them with the designing hand of God.

So the beauty perceived as the intrinsic quality of each thing – its **inscape** – acts as a constantly repeated imaginative proof of the existence of a God who had created that **inscape** and was himself partly reflected in it. More than this, you could argue that when Hopkins wrote a poem, he was attempting through its form and language to reproduce the sense of **inscape** he found in the world around him. God was responsible for the (concealed) essence of each thing Hopkins saw; glimpsing this **inscape** reinforced Hopkins's sense of the beauty of the being who created it all; the poem then became an attempt to find words and rhythms capable of evoking for others the writer's sense of divine energy.

All of which leads on, inevitably, to a demanding group of texts where the eternal dramas of salvation matter to Hopkins even more than his deep feeling for the beauty of nature. Reading Hopkins involves all the factors explored so far in these Interpretations, but it also involves something darker, arguably far less accessible. And what that might be is taken up in the following section.

Hopkins's religious beliefs

Thy Terror, O Christ, O God

The image, so far: a voice, original, experimental, full of energetic rhythms and vivid language; preoccupied with the music of poetry, the aural effects of echo, rhyme, alliteration. The voice seems intoxicated with the freshness and variety of nature. It celebrates the creative energies alongside the created beauties; it projects a springtime image of a world of enamelled perfection, created for our pleasure by an all-powerful God. This world is *charged with the grandeur of God* (*God's Grandeur* [1]); pregnant with *all this juice and all this joy* (*Spring* [9]). Indeed, when confronted by the full range of the creation, *All things counter, original, spare, strange* (*Pied Beauty* [7]) Hopkins automatically reflects on its maker: *He fathers-forth whose beauty is past change* (*Pied Beauty* [10]). It is no great surprise that the inevitable response is one of reverence and worship: *Praise him* (*Pied Beauty* [11]).

But this is a partial image. All is not sweetness and light. In the Christian understanding as Hopkins himself endorsed it, humanity came to the world as the apex of the creative enterprise, created in God's own likeness, but the free will which God allowed humans also allowed the possibility of sin. And with sin came transience, death, decay.

It is significant that even in one of the most celebratory of the 'nature' poems, the sonnet *Spring*, the idyllic vision conveyed in the octet is described in the sestet as *A strain of the earth's sweet being in the beginning/In Eden garden* (10–11). In regarding spring as a glimpse back into something irretrievably lost, the state of innocence and perfection which existed before sin brought death into nature, Hopkins reminds us that his sense of beauty is not something naïve or myopic, divorced from the darker realities of our human experience.

The theological context: original sin

For Hopkins, the original sin which all humanity has inherited from Adam leaves us sinful and liable to punishment from God as the perfect embodiment of justice. But as a Christian, Hopkins also believes that we can be spared this deserved punishment through divine mercy, since God is also the perfect embodiment of love. So the sense of God disclosed in his poems involves a delicate balancing act. Hopkins reveres the loving God and trembles in the presence of the just God. This is a classically Christian dialectic, balancing opposed or contradictory concepts: the individual, sensitive to his condition, hoping for an undeserved eternity in paradise from God the loving father, fearful of a wholly deserved eternity in Hell from God the cosmic judge. It is this dramatic spiritual context which gives us the key to the darkest in mood of all Hopkins's poems, the so-called 'Sonnets of Desolation', written towards the end of his life and the longest of his poems, *The Wreck of the Deutschland*.

It was graphic images such as this of the sinking *Deutschland*, in newspapers of the time, which prompted Hopkins's initial thoughts for his most ambitious poem: *The breakers rolled on her beam with ruinous shock* (line 109, pp. 18–29).

Activity

Look at the opening stanza of *The Wreck of the Deutschland*. How similar in technique is it to other texts already discussed? What might you say of the characterization of God in the stanza?

Discussion

The **sprung rhythm** is evident at once. Stresses vary between two (in the first line of the stanza) and six (in the final line). In *Part the first* this gives a stress sequence in each stanza of 2,3,4,3,5,5,4,6. In this opening stanza stresses often fall on single syllable words (*Thou* (1), *me* (1), *breath* (2), *bread* (2)); the effect is to make the rhythm feel energetic. But the energy seems anxious; God, *mastering* (1), is responsible for life, making the poet who he is, but he almost *unmade* (6) him too. The emphatic alliteration contributes both to the urgent rhythm and to the feeling of unease. This quality may also perhaps relate to the use of rhyme; the way three rhymes are used in each eight-line stanza (ababcbca) means that strong sounds at the start of each stanza recur at the end, suggesting the effect of constraint or limitation. The impression offered in this stanza of the poet's attitude to God is probably best revealed by the final word of line 6, *dread*. There is an awareness of obligation to God, alongside an overwhelming impression of divine power. But the idea of divine love is totally absent.

The Wreck of the Deutschland: celebrating providence

The poem offers you both challenge and pleasure. The challenge comes from those passages where Hopkins wishes to articulate complex religious meanings via an idiom whose originality can work against immediate understanding. But the pleasure comes from those areas of the poem where that same idiom is matched with an appropriate content, and the result is the same lyrical fluency identified as a distinctive strength in other poems.

Above all, it is an ambitious poem: in its 280 lines Hopkins can be seen using a particular event as a symbol for a theme he regarded as universal: Christ's redemptive love for sinful, undeserving humanity. In the shorter poems you can see how an underlying theme is disclosed through something concrete and specific: think of *The Windhover, Binsey Poplars, Hurrahing in Harvest*. In each case, reflection on the **inscape** of a natural object or scene triggers in Hopkins's imagination some religious insight about the reality underpinning the world of appearances.

The point here is that Hopkins does not choose an object or scene as the starting point for his poem. Instead, he is inspired by an event: a disaster, a shipwreck involving heavy loss of life. The disaster in turn prompts thoughts about the nature of God's relationship to mankind; thoughts about providence; thoughts about martyrdom; thoughts about the link between human suffering and Christ's suffering. This all makes the conceptual focus of the poem demanding on its readers, since Hopkins assumes a readership knowledgeable about the theological elements of the text (it was originally submitted for publication in the Jesuit magazine *The Month* – and rejected as too difficult). And it must be said that reading is made still more demanding at times by the voice. The tone may be urgent and innovative, but the stressful rhythmic patterns require economy of language, and when this economy is accompanied by coinages and wordplay, the act of reading can sometimes become a painstaking process of sorting clues.

Activity

Read stanza 27 (p. 27) again, more than once, and if possible aloud. Try to catch the sequence of stress patterns indicated above. If you write the stanza out as prose, keeping Hopkins's original words and punctuation, is the meaning made any easier to grasp? What points in the stanza would you single out as causing particular problems?

Discussion

As prose, keeping to Hopkins's words and punctuation but disregarding line breaks, I am struck by the unnatural run of clauses broken up by the heavy punctuation of lines 210–13:

The jading and jar of the cart,
Time's tasking, it is fathers that asking for ease
Of the sodden-with-its sorrowing heart,
Not danger, electrical horror;

If the *jading and jar* (210) is described as *Time's tasking* (211), it is in syntactical terms in apposition to this second phrase, which is the subject of the verb *fathers* (211); so at the start, a 'proper' prose version might read 'It is the jading and jar of the cart, time's tasking, which fathers that asking for ease of...' Putting the stanza into prose only highlights the inversions and reversals of customary order which feature in Hopkins's poetic syntax. But the distortion of the expected order is responsible for only part of the interpretative challenge here. For the full sense of the clauses ending at the semicolon in line 213 to emerge, you have to hold line 210 in your head until *Not danger, electrical horror*, (213) since the whole sequence stands on the relation *Time's tasking* (211)... *fathers* (211)... *Not danger* (213), a vital contrast, explaining that the nun's anguish is the consequence of a long-term spiritual attrition (*Time's tasking* [211]), not the response to the critical situation she finds herself in. So Hopkins's syntax, his approach to the order and sequence of clauses and words, is a possible source of challenge as you read. Here is a simple example of this: I can say that on my own first attempt to make sense of line 211 I was thwarted by the words *it is fathers*, since I read *fathers* as a plural noun rather than a crucially weighted verb! But syntax is not the only hurdle we meet here. The richly alliterative *sodden-with-its sorrowing heart* (212) needs unpacking; the nun's heart is 'wet' with sorrow, the implied metaphor that of tears. *Electrical horror* (213) offers a strong example of Hopkins's taste for the flamboyant, new-minted phrase, but I suspect it is there largely to add some local colour to the otherwise rather naked *danger* (213), and it strikes a curious note – why electrical? There are some potential problems too in the final couplet; partly syntactic (the disjointed clause order), partly the consequence of compactness, the omission of everyday words like 'is' and 'the'. That said, the surging alliteration of line 216 gives a powerful sense of the poem's intermittent storm music through the six stressed accents (*Burden... wind's... burly... endragonèd seas*), while that final image of the *endragonèd seas* (216) compensates for much of the preceding obscurity.

Inscape and structure

In exploring an event here rather than an object or scene, Hopkins is taking on a subject inherently more dynamic and so stronger in dramatic potential. The claim has been made that Hopkins is attempting in each of his poems to articulate the **inscape** of its subject. If that claim is valid, what can be said about **inscape** in relation to *The Wreck of the Deutschland*?

A start might be made by examining structure. The poem is structured in two unequal parts, the first in ten eight-line stanzas, the second in 25 stanzas. There is an immediate and important contrast between the parts: in *Part the first*, we have a sense of the writer's spiritual life and his paradoxical, all-embracing sense of God. The section ends with two stanzas composed like a prayer, where Hopkins returns to the tone of the beginning, a pious believer's anxious address to God. There is violence and energy in the rhythms and language of *Part the first*, but they seem to be provoked by something private and intimate: the poet's own relationship to God.

By contrast, *Part the second* takes us straight to the situation referred to in the poem's title, something dramatic in the physical world, an event involving terror, distress, loss of life. It is a December night. A ship sailing from Germany to the United States loses its bearing and is grounded on a sandbank in the Thames estuary off the Essex coast. Conditions are appalling: high seas, snow driven on an east-north-easterly gale. Among the passengers are five German nuns, driven to find exile in the United States by the harsh anti-Catholic laws established by German chancellor Bismarck and implemented by his minister Falck (hence the reference in the poem's dedication). Of the two hundred plus passengers on board, over a quarter are drowned, including the nuns. One is reported to have cried out 'O Christ, Christ, come quickly!' (see stanza 24, p. 26) before succumbing to exhaustion and dying in the icy North Sea waters. So, what about **inscape**?

Here is one possibility. *Part the second* narrates the fate of the ship and those on board, but it is in no respect simply a narrative. Indeed, Hopkins was at pains to make clear his own view that the whole poem is not a narrative but an ode: a poem taking a place, person or event as the initial stimulus for a process of reflection. In a letter to Robert Bridges, dated 2 April 1878, Hopkins confessed that *The Deutschland would be more generally interesting if there were more wreck and less discourse, I know, but it is still an ode and not primarily a narrative.* The need here is to integrate the narrative elements in the poem, generally recognizable by their greater immediacy or impact, into Hopkins's larger design. You might pick out in this context stanzas 11–17, 19, 24. The **inscape** may start from narration of an event, but it also needs to refer to the reflective portions of the text, what Hopkins calls in his letter the *discourse*.

For Hopkins the event presented a mystery, a religious difficulty. The nuns, already persecuted in Germany, meet a terrible death on board the intended means of their escape. A black irony? Fate playing a cruel hand? For Hopkins, Fate, blind destiny, was part of the mythological apparatus of paganism, of Greek tragedy. Instead, as a Christian, his own faith was centred on what stanza 31 calls *lovely-felicitous Providence* (245). But what is so lovely about a design for the world which allows five women who have dedicated their lives to the service of God, just as Hopkins did himself, to suffer the agonies of death by shipwreck?

Activity

Look up the word *felicitous* (245) in a dictionary. If you need to, check also on the meaning of *Providence* (245). How might the ideas in the words be linked?

Discussion

As noted above, the original sense of 'felicitous' is blissful, happy. The word can however involve two other senses: apt or appropriate, and ingenious, clever. If 'Providence' involves the concept of God's care ('providing') for his creation, his designer's careful concern, you have in the two words the notion of a design, a plan, either apt or clever or both. Clever plans are often plans which contain much more than you see at first. The divine plan for humans is *lovely* (245) but also clever, appropriate – appropriate for humans who are sinners, who have a right only to punishment? The more you look at the phrase, the more you may come to feel it is saying something at the heart of Hopkins's perceptions in this poem.

Inscape, design, providence: 'Lightning and Love'

The poet who composed *The Wreck of the Deutschland* accepts that there is a problem in reconciling divine love and divine power. The event provoking the poem seems to demonstrate far more of the latter than of the former. But Hopkins's faith turns a problem into a mystery, a sense of the ultimate goodness of the divine plan which cannot be explained or justified on wholly rational grounds. What the entire text might be seen as encapsulating then is the believer's sense of that mystery; the **inscape** Hopkins wants to evoke throughout the poem is his deep intuition that pain and death finally make sense in, are not contradictions of, a universe created and sustained by a loving God.

Within his contradictory experience of God, Hopkins's faith tells him that *Providence* is *lovely-felicitous* (245), despite contrary appearances. But this cannot be demonstrated logically, since there are no rational proofs; the **inscape** discovered in the loss of the ship is the creative good that underpins even such seeming evils as suffering and loss of innocent life. The prayerful tone at the end of stanza 9 (p. 21) offers one clue, itself full of paradoxical ideas, to this suggested **inscape**:

> Beyond saying sweet, past telling of tongue,
> Thou art lightning and love, I found it, a winter and warm;
> Father and fondler of heart thou hast wrung;
> Hast thy dark descending and most art merciful then.   69–72

If the feeling here is linked to the thought developed towards the end of the poem, particularly in stanzas 32–3, this explanation of the poem's underlying purpose – as the disclosure by Hopkins of the **inscape** of divine providence he has painfully glimpsed in the wreck of the ship – may start to make more sense. It is by no means the only way of reading and responding to the text, but it does allow you to think about linking narrative and reflective elements. It also offers a bridge between Hopkins's concerns and technique in this poem and those already examined in some of the sonnets and shorter poems.

The 'Sonnets of Desolation': voicing despair

In a sequence of sonnets written approximately a decade after *The Wreck of the Deutschland*, Hopkins can be seen looking urgently for another kind of **inscape**, attempting to make sense of his own spiritual suffering. The exhilarating prayerful tones with which stanza 35 concludes that poem in celebratory style have disappeared; here the poet's own pain is the inescapable subject, and it is an experience where he finds little sense of divine consolation, no trace of *lovely-felicitous Providence*.

Activity

Look again at the sonnets *'No worst'* (p. 56) and *'I wake and feel'* (p. 55). Concentrate particularly in each on the sestets, lines 9–14. What can you say about tone in these lines, and do you find any links between tone and technique here?

Discussion

The emotional landscape of both poems is dark and threatening. In each case the octet dramatizes the poet's extreme mental distress, while the sestet seems to take a tentative step back, offering an instant of reflection. In *'No worst'*, Hopkins conveys something of the horrors of isolation, picturing himself dizzy with vertigo in an 'alpine' mental landscape. What small relief he finds is bleakness itself; there is at least the nightly oblivion of sleep and the final oblivion of death. And in *'I wake and feel'*, this sobriety is mixed with a caustic dose of self-disgust; he loathes himself, identifying this powerful self-loathing (itself suicidal in tone?) with divine punishment. In this sestet the use of the personal pronoun (*I, me*) emphasizes the sense of isolation. Hell defined not as 'other people' (as the French writer J.-P. Sartre famously expressed it) but as oneself, the mind left alone to contemplate its own inadequacy and failure. This bitter musing on 'self' also reminds me strongly of the powerful lines cited in the Context section at the start of this book, where Hopkins writes of *that taste of myself* – self-consciousness as the most overwhelming part of our mental awareness. In the prose reflection Hopkins's tone is filled with wonder and reverence: by contrast the tone here is unremittingly downcast, even morbid. Linked to this, in both poems I notice the absence of the playful element in earlier texts: the proliferation of inventions, compounds and sound chimes. The tone is severe, the technique appropriately disciplined and channelled to mirror this.

Why this black tone? If these are the poems *written in blood* to which Hopkins made a tantalizing reference in a letter to Bridges of May 1885, what can explain the mood change from earlier texts to this sequence of poems variously described by later commentators as 'the Sonnets of Desolation', 'the terrible sonnets' or "the dark sonnets"? A possible explanation is offered quite explicitly in one of these texts (see Notes to *'To seem the stranger'* p. 103).

Do the language, syntax and rhythms employed in these poems help you to feel the sense of despair experienced by the *I* of the poems? Or do they instead give you a feeling of artifice, of something posed, melodramatic, an exercise in conveying extreme states of dejection? And what part might the voice explored earlier have in this? If the playful elements are conspicuously absent, what remains is the compactness or economy of style, the tense sytax, which so often operates as an infallible voice print in Hopkins.

Activity

Look at the octet of the sonnet (*Carrion Comfort*) (p. 58). How far might it be seen to bear out the critical points made in the last sentence above?

Discussion

The suggestion is that in these late sonnets one ingredient of the voice – the fondness for sound play, echo chains – has largely vanished; what remains characteristic is the compact syntax, the 'jumps' in sense which the reader needs to make in establishing meaning in the text.

In these eight lines there is still evidence of sound play, interest in the sensuous aural pleasure of sound clusters – a consistent trait in Hopkins. Look for instance at the vigorously alliterative sequence in line 6 with *r* and *l* sounds uppermost in the pattern. Similar alliterative patterns occur in the following lines, while assonantal rhyme (vowel sounds) is used internally in the *me... me... thee... flee* sequence of line 8; all quite consistent with the account already offered of the vocal qualities in Hopkins's earlier poems (see p. 142–47). But now the music seems less exuberant and more intense; the six stresses per line of the **sprung rhythm** create a longer, more emphatic effect. This heavier stress pattern is particularly noticeable in lines 1–4, where the sequence of repeated negatives helps to reinforce a feeling of struggle, of grim determination to hang on.

The syntax of these first four lines is direct; there is little of the sense jumping or strange ordering of clauses which occurs in lines 5–8. Here, the syntax offers me a disconnected phrase order needing repeated readings for the underlying sense to emerge. Think about the placing of the adverb *rude* in line 5, or the sense of the words *me frantic* in the second half of line 8. What earlier phrases do you need to keep in mind to make sense of the interrogative *lay a lionlimb against me?* in line 6? All of these examples highlight features of the voice which result from a powerful need in Hopkins to create stylistic originality and distinctiveness through economy, omission, exaggerated attention to non-standard word order (the syntax issue). Hence, cumulatively, the idea of the unique voice print.

The voice, its themes and its range

Earlier poems in the selection have celebrated the natural world in a way special to Hopkins, but within a long tradition of lyric poetry where lightly-stressed rhythms combine with vividly descriptive sounds and imagery to evoke a sense of the writer's joyful encounters with nature. Like the creator God of Genesis, the lyrical Hopkins surveyed the beauty of nature and saw that it was good (Genesis 1:10). Such poems as *Pied Beauty* (p. 35), *God's Grandeur* (p. 31), *Spring* (p. 32) and perhaps most of all, *The Windhover* (p. 34), provide compelling evidence for this point of view.

With *The Wreck of the Deutschland* another dimension is introduced: within the acknowledged beauty of nature, there is a constant dynamic, growth and decay, birth and death, creation and destruction. And for Hopkins, the drama of humanity is at the centre of this universal dynamic: humanity as the creation so loved by the creator that he sacrificed himself to give it a chance of paradise. Encompassing both good and evil, light and dark, the sense of nature in these texts is celebratory; throughout, you can argue that light triumphs in the grand design planned and executed by a loving creator. So lyrical and dramatic elements arguably combine in *The Wreck of the Deutschland* to offer an upbeat vision where human suffering and death are justified by an ultimately confident faith.

But in these later sonnets just discussed, that upbeat vision is absent. There is a strong element of drama: Hopkins articulates feelings of hurt and loss, he is the rejected lover. Unable to accept estrangement from his beloved, he cannot reconcile himself to a life devoid of meaning or purpose. He feels suicidal; he talks of his *sad self* (2), his *tormented mind* (3) (see the sonnet 'My own *heart'* (p. 59). If it makes any sense to talk of **inscape** in this context, then what the poems focus on is that underlying emotional reality of pain which results when the writer feels his relationship with God no longer inspires or animates him. Whether you regard the factors giving rise to these sonnets as spiritual crisis or nervous collapse (or both) is irrelevant; they expand our sense of Hopkins the poet, offering graphic images of emotional and psychological distress to set against those joyful, exultant **inscapes** of physical nature through which Hopkins first discovered his distinct voice. It turns out to be a voice capable of a far wider emotional range than might be suggested from a first, cursory look at his two earlier nature sonnets *Pied Beauty* or *Spring*.

Conclusion – how good a poet is Hopkins?

Hopkins was not a professional writer, in the sense that a professional writer earns his living from having his work published. He was a Catholic priest, a Jesuit, who died prematurely from complications after an attack of typhoid at the age of 45, having exhausted himself through a gruelling vocation of parish work and teaching. His poems were known only to a small number of admirers, one of whom, the poet Robert Bridges, collected, edited and published a number of them in 1918, nearly thirty years after Hopkins's death. His reputation as a poet is thus almost wholly posthumous.

Bridges on Hopkins: a double-edged interpretation

The tone in which Robert Bridges writes of his late friend's poems is distinctly apologetic and defensive. He talks in an Introduction to Hopkins's poems of his *natural eccentricity*, defined as *a love for subtlety and uncommonness*. It is just possible that you may regard these qualities as virtues or strengths in a writer; Bridges did not, using the emotive word *injured* to describe the effect he felt such characteristics had on Hopkins's poetry. Elsewhere, he returns to this notion of oddness in Hopkins, with the comment that it was *an idiosyncrasy of this student's mind to push everything to its logical extreme, and take pleasure in a paradoxical result.*

Interestingly, Hopkins himself had commented to Bridges in a letter of 1879:

No doubt my poetry errs on the side of oddness... But as air, melody, is what strikes me most of all in music and design in painting, so design, pattern or what I am in the habit of calling inscape is what I above all aim at in poetry. Now it is the virtue of design, pattern or inscape to be distinctive and it is the vice of distinctiveness to become queer. This vice I cannot have escaped.

Bridges's suggestion seems to be that finding pleasure in paradoxes is somehow immoral, or at least not respectable. But what about the argument that paradox (a statement or idea which seems to involve violent contradictions) is at the heart of Hopkins's view of the world, particularly as depicted in *The Wreck of the Deutschland*? Significantly, it is Bridges who refers to this poem in his Preface to the 1918 first edition as *the great dragon coiled in the gate to forbid entrance,* as if it were something obviously daunting or inhibiting for potential readers.

He then itemizes the stylistic lapses identified in Hopkins's technique. The manner is reminiscent of an old-fashioned teacher censuring a wayward student's writing (some features are described as *definite faults of style*). His reservations are not confined to style and grammar, however. In looking at *The Blessed Virgin compared to the Air we Breathe*, he criticizes its *exaggerated Marianism* (see Notes). He refers disparagingly to *the naked encounter of sensualism and asceticism which hurts The Leaden Echo and The Golden Echo.* Notice *hurts*; like *injured* the word suggests painful damage, a living organism affected by its creator's defects in matters of style and judgement.

When such negative points are set in a context where Bridges still wishes to highlight the beauty and insights he finds in Hopkins's poetry, we have an overall assessment which is, to say the least, mixed: the admiration is both qualified and puzzled. Bridges talks of the poems as if the appropriate criteria for response were those of polite manners or etiquette; there is a revealing comment in his Preface that Hopkins's style involves *a neglect of those canons of taste which seem common to all poetry.* Hopkins displays indifference to the implicit ideal of simplicity. The mannered, wilfully inventive idiom thereby not only qualifies any chance Hopkins has of becoming a 'classic' in the English literary canon; it is also an affront, intended or otherwise, to poetic decency.

Bridges saw much of Hopkins's stylistic originality as idiosyncratic, differing radically and unacceptably from tradition. Later readers have seen this quality in Hopkins as the essence of his achievement, what makes reading him a special and worthwhile experience. For Bridges and other Victorian readers, Hopkins failed to keep the right balance between innovation and tradition. By contrast, readers since have listened to the poet's voice explored here as something daring and intense; a voice singing a new music that conveys insights about the **inscapes** of physical nature, religious experience, the relation of creator to creation.

Hopkins the original

Hopkins is one of the very few genuinely original poet-experimenters in English, with an idiom wholly and unmistakably his own. He is a writer in whom to a very marked degree inventive technique is matched by inventive thought. He is original, and complex, because he has original and complex things to say, and he is driven to formulate what he says in a style complementing the vision behind it. The argument is that

Hopkins is a visionary. Like all visionaries, his art offers a challenging mixture of images immediately felt to be important alongside a boldness of technique that forces us to read on his terms rather than our own. The results in this selection can certainly be described as uneven; you may perhaps agree with Bridges that perfect integration of voice, form and theme happens quite rarely in the poems, yet the unevenness of the achievement should not be used to diminish its scale in those texts where the voice and its message are in harmony.

Reading Hopkins then is not easy, because it is not meant to be easy – but it can be a moving and exhilarating experience. There is the sense of a mind intoxicated by nature and the creator behind it, for Hopkins more beautifully alive even than nature itself. With such great themes to develop, it is no surprise that this voice can sometimes pose problems in reading. Yet however irregular and obscure the syntax may become, the abiding core is the compelling sense of **inscape**: the formative beauty within all created things, above all in human beings. For Hopkins, we humans are the chief paradox of nature: body yet soul, mortal yet immortal, sinners yet made in the image of God. That vision of our own complex and bewildering **inscape** is realized most powerfully at the close of one of his finest and most characteristic poems, a sonnet that extends sonnet form far beyond the traditional parameters as Bridges and his contemporaries would understand them. With its sense of drama, its rhythmic energy and its alliterative music, the climax of *That Nature is a Heraclitean Fire and of the comfort of the Resurrection* epitomizes the acute marriage of intellect and feeling that makes Hopkins's best poems utterly distinctive, challenging and moving human documents:

> In a flash, at a trumpet crash,
> I am all at once what Christ is, since he was what I am, and
> This Jack, joke, poor potsherd, patch, matchwood, immortal
>   diamond,
> Is immortal diamond.   (21–4)

Essay Questions

1 A striking feature of Hopkins's prose Journals is the care he takes in describing the natural phenomena he observes. To what extent have you found that interest in observing nature reflected in the poems in this selection? In your answer you should **either** refer to **two** or **three** poems in detail **or** range more widely through the selection.

2 Look again at the sonnet *That Nature is a Heraclitean Fire and of the comfort of the Resurrection* (p. 63). Discuss how far you would consider the poem an extreme example of Hopkins's style and concerns as a poet. Your answer should consider the following aspects:
   • the language and imagery used in the first nine lines
   • the theme of 'resurrection' developed in the latter half of the poem
   • how Hopkins links natural description and religious themes together.

3 'Many readers think of Hopkins as a nature poet – but he only finds nature interesting because it provides constant evidence of the God who created it.' How far do you agree with this judgement?

4 Look again at the sonnets *'To seem the stranger'* (p. 55) and *'I wake and feel'* (p. 55). Explore the ways in which Hopkins conveys frustration and self-disgust in these poems.

5 Hopkins's first editor, Robert Bridges, was critical of *The Wreck of the Deutschland* and described it as *a great dragon coiled in the gate to forbid all entrance*. How far do you consider the style and themes of that poem are important in the context of the poems in this selection that were written subsequently?

6 Remind yourself of stanzas XII–XIX (lines 89–152) of *The Wreck of the Deutschland*. How successfully does Hopkins use language, rhythm and imagery to evoke the situation of the ship and the nuns in this section of the poem?

7 How significant do you think having sympathy for Hopkins's religious beliefs is in responding to his poems? In your answer you should **either** refer to **two** or **three** poems in detail **or** range more widely through the selection.

8 What sense have you gained from this selection of Hopkins's awareness of beauty? Refer to evidence from at least **two** poems in your answer.

9 A critic has recently written that in Hopkins's poems *Women are defined in terms of their connections with, or relationships to, men… Only female lives as seen by Catholic traditions are explored by individual texts…* From your reading of Hopkins does this seem a fair judgement? In your answer you should refer to at least **two** poems.

10 Remind yourself of *The Windhover* (p. 34). How far in terms of its subject matter and technique would you consider it representative of other poems in this selection? In your answer you should refer **either** to **two** or **three** poems in detail **or** range more widely through the selection.

11 Hopkins remarked in a letter that *design, pattern, or what I am in the habit of calling Inscape is what I above all aim at in poetry.* How helpful to your understanding of Hopkins have you found the idea of **inscape**? In your answer you should **either** refer to **two** or **three** poems in detail **or** range more widely through the selection.

Chronology

Year	Hopkins's life and work	Literary, scientific and cultural developments	Social and political events
1844	Born, 28 July, at Stratford in Essex, the oldest of eight children.	Morse invents the telegraph	The first Co-operative Society is established
1845		Engels, *The Condition of the Working Class in England*	Irish potato famine – agitation for Home Rule grows in its aftermath; John Henry Newman converts to Roman Catholicism, causing crisis in the Anglican church
1847		Charlotte Brontë, *Jane Eyre*; Emily Brontë, *Wuthering Heights*	
1848		Marx and Engels, *The Communist Manifesto*; Thackeray, *Vanity Fair*; Dante Gabriel Rossetti, William Holman Hunt and John Everett Millais form the Pre-Raphaelite Brotherhood, a movement aiming to re-vitalize art by returning to 'pure' models as advocated by the critic and artist John Ruskin	'Year of revolutions' across Europe; Chartist Petition (campaign for political rights and wider franchise by working class); first Public Health Act in the wake of cholera epidemic when over 50,000 die
1850		Tennyson, *In Memoriam*; Wordsworth, *The Prelude*; Elizabeth Barrett Browning, *Sonnets from the Portuguese*; natural sciences taught for the first time at Oxford (Cambridge starts the following year); first telegraph cable under English Channel	Catholic hierarchy restored in England; for the first time, Factory Act imposes conditions on hours of work in textiles industry for women and teenage workers
1854	Family having moved to Hampstead in north London, Hopkins attends Highgate School, where he does well academically and wins prizes for his poetry	Holman Hunt's painting *The Light of the World*; John Snow demonstrates that cholera is spread by contaminated water supplies and so founds the science of epidemiology; Tennyson, *The Charge of the Light Brigade*	Crimean War (Britain and France in conflict with the Russian Empire over trading rights in the Middle East)

Year	Hopkins's life and work	Literary, scientific and cultural developments	Social and political events
1855		Robert Browning, *Men and Women*	Abolition of stamp duty on newspapers reduces prices; Florence Nightingale begins hospital reforms
1859		Darwin, *On the Origin of Species*; J. S. Mill, *On Liberty*; Tennyson, *Idylls of the King*	
1860		*Essays and Reviews*, a collection of essays about the Bible attracts controversy because of its authors' belief that the Bible should be interpreted as a set of texts with human authorship; Ruskin, *Modern Painters*	
1863	Enters Balliol College, Oxford, to study 'Greats' (Latin and Greek literature, history and thought)	J. S. Mill, *Utilitarianism*; Charles Lyell, *Antiquity of Man*	Founding of the Salvation Army; first underground railway (Metropolitan Line) opens in London
1864		John Henry Newman's spiritual autobiography, *Apologia pro vita sua*	
1866	Becomes a Catholic, to the great concern of his family; received into Catholic church by John Henry Newman		Sanitary Act – the first law aimed at making local authorities responsible for public health measures
1867	Graduates from Oxford with first-class honours; teaches for eight months at Newman's Oratory School in Birmingham; *Teaching is very burdensome, especially when you have much of it: I have*	Sir Joseph Lister demonstrates carbolic as an antiseptic; Christopher Scholes develops the first practical typewriter; Alfred Nobel produces dynamite; Karl Marx, *Das Kapital*	Disraeli's Second Reform Bill expands electorate to cover the majority of urban working men; Fenian uprising in Ireland; founding of Dominion of Canada (first part of British Empire to achieve political autonomy)

Year	Hopkins's life and work	Literary, scientific and cultural developments	Social and political events
1868	Begins training for the Jesuit priesthood; burns the poems he has already composed (probable explanation for *murder of the innocents* reference in his Journal)	Matthew Arnold, *Selected Poems* (includes *Dover Beach*); St Pancras Station train shed designed by William Barlow, one of the great architectural monuments of 'the railway age'	Last public hangings in Britain; first Trades Union Congress meets in Manchester
1870	Starts three years of philosophy study at Stonyhurst College, Lancs., principal Jesuit school and training college	Dante Gabriel Rossetti, *Poems*	Forster's Education Act establishes minimum state provision for schooling; Vatican Council proclaims doctrine of papal infallibility; Franco-Prussian War results in humiliating defeat for France and the emergence of Prussia under Bismarck as a major European power
1871		Darwin, *The Descent of Man*	Test Act allows non-Anglicans to attend Oxford and Cambridge; Trade Union Act recognizes unions as legal bodies
1872	Discovers the work of Duns Scotus: *from this time I was flush with a new enthusiasm*	George Eliot, *Middlemarch*; Russian chemist Mendeleyev publishes the Periodic Table of elements	Gladstone's Licensing Act introduces restrictions on public house opening hours; introduction of secret ballots for elections
1874	As part of his training, goes to St Beuno's College in North Wales	Hardy, *Far from the Madding Crowd*	
1875	First serious attempt at poetry for seven years – starts to compose *The Wreck of the Deutschland*	Gilbert and Sullivan's *Trial by Jury* staged in London – the first in a series of immensely popular 'Savoy operas'	Britain takes a controlling interest in the Suez Canal (opened 1869)
1877	Writes a number of his most well-known sonnets, including *God's Grandeur*, *The Windhover* and *Pied Beauty*; is ordained and begins teaching work in Chesterfield	Alexander Graham Bell invents the telephone; the first sound recording by Thomas Edison	Charles Parnell becomes leader of Irish Home Rule Party; Queen Victoria is made Empress of India

Year	Hopkins's life and work	Literary, scientific and cultural developments	Social and political events
1878	Sent back to Stonyhurst College as a teacher; writes *The Loss of the Eurydice*; December, to Oxford as curate of parish church		
1880	Posting to poor Liverpool parish of St Francis Xavier; writes *Felix Randal* and *Spring and Fall*		First conflict in South Africa against Boers
1882	Returns to Stonyhurst to teach classics; writes *The Leaden Echo and the Golden Echo*		British officials assassinated, Phoenix Park, Dublin; continued unrest against British rule; Married Women's Property Act gives women the right to their own property after marriage
1884	Last major posting as professor of Greek and Latin literature at University College, Dublin		
1885	Likely period in which the 'Sonnets of Desolation' are composed	Karl Benz develops the first car to exploit internal combustion; Louis Pasteur develops a vaccine against rabies	
1886	Meets the young W. B. Yeats; writes *Spelt from Sybil's Leaves*		Gladstone's Irish Home Rule Bill defeated in the Commons; he resigns
1889	Starts year with spiritual retreat; contracts typhoid; dies, 8 June	Eiffel Tower completed; Dewar and Abel invent cordite, a smokeless explosive	
1918	First edition of Hopkins's poems published by Oxford University Press and edited by Robert Bridges		

Further Reading

Editions

There are two editions of Hopkins's complete poems available in paperback. The first has been the standard edition of the poems for many years:

W. H. Gardner and N. H. Mackenzie (ed.), *The Poems of Gerard Manley Hopkins* (Oxford University Press, 4th ed. 1970).

Catherine Phillips (ed.), *Gerard Manley Hopkins* (Oxford Authors Series, Oxford University Press, 1986).

Not yet in paperback is this scholarly edition of the poems (with variants):

N. H. Mackenzie (ed.), *Poems of Gerard Manley Hopkins* (Oxford University Press, 1990).

Prose Writings

Hopkins's prose writings are worth studying in their own right, and are certainly as readable and as stylish in their own way as the poems. They will add to your sense of Hopkins's personality and outlook, enriching your impression of the mind at work in the poems. The standard edition of Hopkins's letters is in three volumes and in hardback only:

C. C. Abbott (ed.), *Vol. I: The Letters of Gerard Manley Hopkins to Robert Bridges; Vol. II: The Correspondence of Gerard Manley Hopkins with R. W. Dixon; Vol. III: The Further Letters of Gerard Manley Hopkins* (Oxford University Press, 2nd ed. 1955–6).

There is also an attractive selection of letters in paperback which forms part of the Oxford Letters and Memoirs Series:

Catherine Phillips (ed.), *Gerard Manley Hopkins Selected Letters* (Oxford University Press, 1991).

The standard edition of Hopkins's Journals and Papers, which complements the more informal tone of the letters, is again only available in hardback and is probably best sought out in libraries:
H. House and G. Storey (ed.), *The Journals and Papers of Gerard Manley Hopkins* (Oxford University Press, 1959).

If you are interested in the religious dimensions of Hopkins's thinking, you will discover many absorbing reflections and insights in the following (again, only in hardback):
C. Devlin (ed.), *Sermons and Devotional Writings* (Oxford University Press, 1959).

Biography

Hopkins's life, particularly the impact on his creative development of his work as a Jesuit, is covered by this very readable biography in paperback:
Robert Bernard Martin, *Gerard Manley Hopkins – A Very Private Life* (HarperCollins, 1992).

Criticism

In terms of critical writing on the poetry, posterity has certainly made up for the sluggishness with which Hopkins first became known to a wide audience. In the following selection, you will find responses to qualities in the poetry which should stimulate your own thinking.

First, two helpful collections of essays, each in paperback, each with an introduction which helps throw light on the ways critical assessments of Hopkins have evolved over the past half century:
M. Bottrall (ed.), *Gerard Manley Hopkins: Poems* (Casebook Series, Macmillan, 1975).

G. Hartman (ed.), *Hopkins: A Collection of Critical Essays* (Twentieth Century View Series, Prentice Hall, 1966).

NB: The views of the three critics whose readings of *The Windhover* feature early in the Interpretations section of this book can be found in the Bottrall critical anthology; in order, the critics are I. A. Richards, William Empson and Elisabeth Schneider.

The following longer studies of the poetry can be recommended:
G. Storey, *A Preface to Hopkins* (Longman, 1978).
N. H. MacKenzie, *A Reader's Guide to Hopkins* (Thames and Hudson, 1981).
J. R. Watson, *The Poetry of Gerard Manley Hopkins: A Critical Study* (Penguin Masterstudies Series, Penguin, 1987).

Also worth searching out in libraries is W. H. Gardner's *Gerald Manley Hopkins: A Study of Poetic Idiosyncrasy in Relation to Poetic Tradition* (volume one first published in 1944, on the centenary of Hopkins's birth, revised edition published 1958).

The single most influential essay on Hopkins, in terms of its impact on Hopkins's status and in terms of the insight it conveys on the poetry, is probably the chapter devoted to Hopkins in *New Bearings in English Literature* by F. R. Leavis. This was first published by Chatto and Windus in 1932, but has been reprinted in paperback by Penguin frequently since then. It is particularly interesting to read Leavis in the light of Robert Bridges's careful reservations on his late friend's genius.

Robert Bridges's reservations about Hopkins's poetry are cogently developed by the independently minded American critic Yvor Winters in a section of his book:
Yvor Winters, *The Function of Criticism* (reprinted in the Hartman critical anthology mentioned above).

If you are interested in discovering more about the way that critics have evaluated Hopkins's work and so established a 'canon' of views about it, there is a comprehensive collection of reviews and essays covering the period 1918–1940 in the *Critical Heritage* series, edited by Gerald Roberts (RKP, 1987).

The following websites provide a wide range of critical, bibliographical and textual materials on Hopkins, with further links to sites exploring such key elements as his place within Victorian literature, his spirituality and the influence of his Jesuit vocation:

www.dundee.ac.uk/english/hopkins.htm
It includes a very useful concordance, enabling you to trace Hopkins's use of particular words throughout his poems.

www.literaryhistory.com/19thC/HOPKINS.htm

www.victorianweb.org/authors/hopkins/gmhov.html
An excellent site with links to features about many of the different contemporary 'contexts' for Hopkins's writing – literary, scientific, technological, theological, political, etc.

www.bartleby.com/122/
Electronic texts of the poems.

www.gerardmanleyhopkins.org/index.html
Gerald Manley Hopkins Society website – links to articles about Hopkins, his poetry and the religious context of his work.

The following three sites provide more detail about the social context of the age in which Hopkins lived:

www.learningcurve.gov.uk/index/default1750.htm
A basic but highly informative National Archives education site with some entertaining interactive pages.

www.victoriantimes.org/
A lively site developed by Strathclyde University, and allowing research into many aspects of the Victorian world on a number of different levels.

www.bbc.co.uk/history/programmes/victorians
An accessible BBC site including material on many social aspects of Victorian England.

If you are looking for a critical challenge, the following link is to an essay published in 2004 that uses *The Windhover* as a case study in the variety of ways we are conditioned to interpret imagery, specifically allegory, in literary texts:

poeticstoday.dukejournals.org/cgi/content/refs/25/3/437

Index of Titles and First Lines